Religion, Development and African Identity

Seminar Proceedings No 17

Religion, Development and African Identity

Edited by
Kirsten Holst Petersen

Scandinavian Institute of African Studies
Uppsala 1987

SEMINAR PROCEEDINGS FROM THE SCANDINAVIAN INSTITUTE OF
AFRICAN STUDIES

1. Soviet Bloc, China and Africa. Eds. Sven Hamrell and C.G. Widstrand. 173 pp. Uppsala 1964. (Out-of-print)
2. Development and Adult Education in Africa. Ed. C.G. Widstrand. 97 pp. Uppsala 1965. (Out-of-print)
3. Refugee Problems in Africa. Ed. Sven Hamrell. 123 pp. Uppsala 1967. Skr. 10:-
4. The Writer in Modern Africa. Ed. Per Wästberg. 123 pp. Uppsala 1968. Skr 15:-
5. African Boundary Problems. Ed. C.G. Widstrand. 202 pp. Uppsala 1969. Skr 15:-
6. Cooperatives and Rural Development in East Africa. Ed. C.G. Widstrand. 271 pp. Uppsala 1970. (Out-of-print)
7. Reporting Africa. Ed. Olav Stokke. 223 pp. Uppsala 1971. Skr 30:-
8. African Cooperatives and Efficiency. Ed. C.G. Widstrand. 239 pp. Uppsala 1972. Skr. 30:-
9. Land-locked Countries of Africa. Ed. Zdenek Červenka. 368 pp. Uppsala 1973. Skr. 40:-
10. Multinational Firms in Africa. Ed. C.G. Widstrand. With an introduction by Samir Amin. 425 pp. Uppsala 1975. (Out-of-print)
11. African Refugees and the Law. Eds. Göran Melander and Peter Nobel. 98 pp. Uppsala 1978. Skr. 40:-
12. Problems of Socialist Orientation in Africa. Ed. Mai Palmberg. 243 pp. Uppsala 1978. (Out-of-print)
13. Canada, Scandinavia and Southern Africa. Eds. D. Anglin, T. Shaw and C.G. Widstrand 190 pp. Uppsala 1978. Skr. 70:-
14. South-South Relations in a Changing World Order. Ed. Jerker Carlsson. 166 pp. Uppsala 1982. Skr. 90:-
15. Recession in Africa. Ed. Jerker Carlsson. 203 pp. Uppsala 1983. Skr. 95:-
16. Land Management and Survival. Ed. Anders Hjort. 148 pp. Uppsala 1985. Skr. 100:-
17. Religion, Development and African Identity. Ed. Kirsten Holst Petersen. 163 pp. Uppsala 1987. Skr. 110:-

ISSN 0281-0018
ISBN 91-7106-263-7

Printed in Sweden by
Ekblad & Co, Västervik, 1987

Contents

Preface

Carl F Hallencreutz

Religion, Development and African Identity was the theme of a six-day conference, jointly arranged by the Scandinavian Institute of African Studies (SIAS) and the Nordic Institute of Missionary Research (NIME) in Uppsala, Sweden, 16th to 21st August 1984. The main issues explored are reflected in this collection of essays and papers. The theme of this conference was further pursued at the sixth Third-annual Congress of the International Association of Mission Studies (IAMS), held in Harare, Zimbabwe, January 1985. There the President of Zimbabwe, Canaan Banana lectured on the Church's mission in a socialist state. In his presentation President Banana summarized his views on Church and State, which he had previously expounded in his book, *Theology of Promise. The Dynamics of Self-Reliance* (Harare 1982). The frank and open discussion which followed the presentation raised social-ethical and exegetical problems, such as how the President interpreted the saying "give God what belongs to God and Caesar what belongs to Caesar". The President was evidently intellectually stimulated by the reactions as he made a number of perceptive observations.

This session was closed by a very thought-provoking exchange of views between the Anglican Bishop of Mashonaland, the Rt. Rev. Peter Hatendi, and the former Methodist pastor, President Banana. Bishop Hatendi suggested that there are no real problems in the Church's interaction with Socialism. Problems may, however, emerge when Government officials begin to plead for "Scientific Socialism". President Banana suggested that religion is a basic reality in any African society and has as such to be considered in any development strategy relevant to Africa. Scientific socialism according to the President could, therefore, not mean anti-religious materialism. Instead, it stood for a rational - or scientific - testing of the appropriate means to achieve agreed political objectives.

This exchange of views on contemporary Church-State relations in Africa between two distinguished Zimbabwean Comrades illustrates the necessary interaction of Religion and Development in Africa. The discussion between Bishop Hatendi and President Banana also highlights certain dimensions of what has been termed African Identity.

It is this complexity that NIME and SIAS desired to touch upon through the conference theme *Religion, Development and African Identity*. It soon became evident that the real issue was what African identity may imply. It is easy to prove that when we speak of Religion and Development in contemporary Africa, we refer to three major religious traditions: the indigenous African tradition in its manifold expressions; the Muslim and the Christian faiths. We discussed how they interact with each other in countries which pursue different development strategies and different policies towards religion. When we look more closely at this interaction, however, we realize that differences within these traditions are quite significant. Dr Paulo Farias of Birmingham, Great Britain, and Professor Sven Rubensson of Lund, Sweden, reminded the participants that these differences within and between both Christianity and Islam have a long and varied history in Africa.

Development, too, is a multidimensional phenomenon, which can be seen from many points of view. This was highlighted very effectively by Professor Marja-Liisa Swantz from Helsinki, Finland, in her paper with reference to African women in socio-economic change and cultural and religious transformation. Professor Swantz also raised the basic question, as to whether it is possible to speak of an African identity in general terms, or if one should not differentiate between identities which are socially and economically, as well as culturally and religiously, conditioned.

As a research seminar within NIME's sphere of interest the joint conference focussed particularly on the role of Christianity in African development - and, perhaps, as an expression of African identity. It is interesting to note that the different contributions in this book illustrate different methodological perspectives and research emphases in the study of African Christianity and its history.

The introduction to the theme of the conference was a panel discussion between Professors Marja-Liisa Swantz and Terence Ranger (from Manchester, Great Britain) and Miss Agnes Chepkwony, PhD student in Mission Studies in Uppsala.

Professor Ranger also read a paper, which together with that of Dr Moyo's, gave an interesting account of present Church-state relations in Zimbabwe. The steering committee also asked Professor Ranger to sum up and critically assess the work of the conference. Both Zimbabwe papers and Professor Ranger's witty and thought-provoking analysis of the exchange of ideas during the conference are presented in this volume.

The collected papers, thus, communicate the substance of the joint SIAS-NIME conference on *Religion, Development and African Identity* in Uppsala. However, what is presented here is not a complete documentation. The editorial committee has not found it necessary to report on the discussions in the topical and regional groups. The focus there was on current research projects which will be presented either in special reports or as forthcoming PhD theses. Nor do we include, for instance, Bishop Patrick Kalilombe's (from Birmingham, Great Britain) personal presentation of the charismatic archbishop and healer, the Most Reverend E. Milingo of Lusaka and Rome. Only an appended video-casette would have done the presentation justice!

In presenting these papers we hope that they will inspire continued informed interest in issues relating to religion, development and African identity. This would correspond with the objectives of those who contributed to make the seminar a success. It would also be in accord with the expectations of those who made the conference and this report financially viable, and to whom our thanks are due.

The Shattered Microcosm: A Critical Survey of Explanations of Conversion in Africa

Emefie Ikenga-Metuh

The phenomenon of "conversion" in Africa has attracted the attention of social scientists and historians of religion for many reasons, the most striking of which is its phenomenal dimensions. After several unsuccessful attempts in the past to plant Christianity in Africa, the numbers of Christians in Africa increased to over 160 million in little more than one hundred years of evangelization. A similar growth has been recorded for Islam.[1] Both religions have grown in extent and numbers more rapidly and successfully in the last fifty years than at any previous period of their long history.[2] Firstly, the drift is from African Traditional Religions to the two major world religions - Christianity and Islam. Secondly, this period of massive conversion corresponded with a period of rapid socio-cultural change - colonialism, industrialization, and modernization - which swept Africa into the mainstream of world activity. Thirdly, for Christianity, and to a lesser extent for Islam, the phenomenal increase in the numbers of adherents was accompanied by an equally unprecedented mushrooming of indigenous church movements. According to Barret, there are about eight thousand such Afro-Christian churches in Africa which between them have over fourteen million adherents.[3]

Any explanation of the phenomenon of conversion in Africa must answer a number of crucial questions: What are the reasons for this massive move from African traditional religions to Islam and Christianity? If this mass conversion indeed came in the wake of colonialism and rapid socio-cultural change, what if any is the causal link between them? To what extent could this religious change be called "conversion"? Finally, what is the explanation of the high incidence of independent Afro-Christian church movements?

Explanations given for this movement from traditional religions to Christianity and Islam in Africa during this period can roughly be grouped into four categories: i) The Shattered Microcosm, ii) The Intellectualist

Theory, iii) A Historical Explanation, and iv) A Socio-Structural Explanation. The task of this essay is to make a critical analysis of each of these explanations. Following from this, the essay then suggests that "conversion" in Africa, as a socio-cultural as well as a religio-social change, is a multi-causal phenomenon and cannot be explained exclusively by any one of the theories proposed. Rather, I would argue that the factors are many and varied. It is not only the response of traditional tribal cultures to modernization, but also a response of Africans and African Religions to Islam and missionary Christianity.

THE SHATTERED MICROCOSM

Trimingham attributes the move from traditional religions to Christianity and Islam to the collapse of the structures of traditional African societies and African world-views - the Shattered Microcosm. The sudden impact of Western civilization in the form of colonial subjugation and domination, technological superiority, industrial economy and education, upset the social structures of African societies, based as they were on tribal structures and rural subsistence economies. African traditional religions are so bound up with their social structures that the collapse of the latter also precipitated the collapse of religious life. "Decay and disruption threaten the ethnic and local religions as never before just because they are so integrally one with the local community". Trimingham concludes:

> The indigenous religions, being primarily local and ethnic, have no future in their organized forms, and the religious future of the African today lies between Christianity and Islam, on the one hand, and secularism on the other. His choice is between religions which lay claim to universality, whether positive or negative in their approach to live values.[4]

He reasons that as African Traditional Religions are ethnic religions, they are only relevant to small-scale clan societies and rural village life rather than modern urban life.

> Village religion is serviceable only within the circumscribed bounds of village life. When horizons were widened, its limitations were felt, and this led many to adopt either Islam or Christianity parallel to those aspects of the old religions which are still serviceable.[5]

The proliferation of Afro-Christian churches according to Trimingham was due to the intolerance of missionary Christianity, and the tendency of new converts to introduce elements of their traditional religion into Christianity. Islam, he says, was more tolerant of these syncretic tendencies by its converts than Christianity, so that "the animist in his new Islamic garb can make the best of both worlds and find a place within the new society".[6] Conversely, the official refusal of Christianity to tolerate "mixing" among its converts led to the formation of breakaway groups.

Nobody can dispute the fact that the rapid social change that came in the wake of colonialism shattered the structures of traditional societies which had previously sustained traditional religions. Nor can anyone contest the fact that traditional world-views needed to change considerably in order to cope with the much enlarged world to which they were now exposed. Adherents of African religions turned to Islam and Christianity as a convenient means of coping with the changed situation. This could hardly be described as conversion. Trimingham underscores this fact by observing that the average African convert retained some of his traditional beliefs in spite of strong disapproval either from his church, or, if he was a Muslim, from the formal condemnation of this by Islam. It may be necessary therefore to define "conversion" in order to determine what sort of religious change took place in an African who adopted Christianity under the circumstance described by Trimingham, and what factors influenced his decision.

THE INTELLECTUALIST EXPLANATION

The most stimulating attempt to explain the phenomenon of conversion in Africa, and certainly one which has provoked a storm of reactions in the 1970s, is Horton's intellectualist explanation. He took as his point of departure Peel's book, *Aladura: A Religious Movement among the Yoruba* , in which the latter gave an intellectualist explanation of the Aladura Independent Church movement as an attempt to reinterpret and adapt traditional Yoruba cosmology to explain, predict and control events in a new, unfamiliar and changed social situation resulting from the modernization process.[7]

Horton's thesis is that the conversion from African Traditional Religions to Christianity or Islam is as much due to the development of traditional African cosmology responding to features of the modern situation, as it is to the activities of the missionaries. The typical traditional African cosmology, argues Horton, is characterized by a two-tiered arrangement of spiritual beings. In the first tier are the lesser spirits, concerned with the local community and its environment - the microcosm. In the second tier is the Supreme Being, concerned with the whole world - the macrocosm. In pre-Christian and pre-Islamic traditional religions, many beliefs and practices were concerned with techniques for manipulating the lesser spirits, under-pinners of the microcosm, while ideas of the Supreme Being were un-elaborated and dormant, because pre-modern African life was lived out in the microcosm of the village community.

Horton then suggested a "thought experiment" in which he tries to con-front traditional religion with the modern situation - massive development, commerce, and national states, without Christian or Muslim missionary activity. The response of the African world-view he argues, would be to develop the concept of the Supreme Being, to meet the challenges of the macrocosm while reducing in importance the lesser spirits, underpinners of the microcosm. Thus a people seeing the boundary of the microcosm weakening or dissolving, can only interpret these changes by assuming that the lesser spirits (underpinners of the microcosm) are in retreat, and that the Supreme Being (underpinner of the macrocosm) is taking direct control. People would then begin to develop a more elaborate cult of the Supreme Being and a moral code closely linked with the Supreme Being.

Horton concludes that it would appear that the beliefs and practices of the so called world religions are only accepted where they happen to coincide with changes in traditional cosmology relating to other, non-missionary, factors in the modern situation. Such a situation, he concludes, reduces Islam and Christianity to the role of catalysts - stimulators and "accelerators of changes which were in the air anyway."[8]

Horton goes on to explain the proliferation of Independent churches in much the same way as Trimingham does. Whereas Islam has accepted the catalyst role by allowing the individual to make his own particular selection from official doctrines, missionary Christianity has never been content to play the catalyst role. Its insistence that each individual accepts all Christian doctrines, while renouncing all others, has resulted in the proliferation of breakaway sects.[9]

Attractive and well-argued as Horton's hypothesis may seem, it has provoked many critical reactions. However, immediately evident is the similarity between Horton's and Trimingham's explanations. In fact Horton's arguments on closer examination are not more than Trimingham's explanation cast in an intellectualist frame. Both share the view that the adoption of Christianity and Islam is the inevitable consequence of the crumbling of the structures of traditional society. Both agree that the traditional world-views of the microcosm in the rural village world are inoperable in the macrocosm. Both, I think, would share the view that the adoption of Islam or Christianity was precipitated by the changed situation, which their traditional world-view could not incorporate, and not necessarily because they accepted the beliefs of either world religion. The desire to retain their own beliefs despite missionary opposition often resulted in the founding of Afro-Christian churches. The impression one gets from Trimingham's analysis is that adherents of African Religions turned to Islam and Christianity as a convenient means of coping with a changed situation. The impulse to embrace either religion may well have come from missionary propaganda or from the adaptive potential of traditional religion, but this does not immediately come through from his analysis. Horton, on the other hand, took this argument further. While not denying the contribution of missionary work, he argues that the change was triggered off by the response of the traditional world-view to the modernization process, and could have resulted in a monolatric cult with or without Christianity or Islam. It is this last claim which many find a pill too strong to swallow.

Horton's explanation was greeted with enthusiasm by many Africanists who shared an ideological committment to essential continuity in African societies, and the capacity of the African to shape and reshape his own social and ritual world, instead of being the mere recipient of ideas and commodities from Western sources.[10] Others understandably are not convinced by his arguments. Fisher, for example, observed that there is no "sound historical reason for expecting that adherents of African traditional faiths will behave as Horton's thought-experiment suggests - that they can only interpret changes in their society in a particular way, that they necessarily evolve a monotheistic moral code for the wider world."[11] Ifeka-Moller has a similar reservation. "In effect", she complains, "Horton is saying: we know that monolatric shifts in traditional cult would have taken place (minus Christianity) because of what actually did happen historically (plus Christianity)."[12] Fisher cited the cases of a number of African societies which were exposed to the macrocosm and which did not develop monolatric cults by themselves without Christianity.

In fact it is fallacious to argue from the prediction of how traditional world-views would react to modernization in the event of an encounter (hypothetically framed), and then conclude that it did in fact react that way in all historical encounters. This sort of infallible prediction would be more understandable if claimed for physical and chemical compounds rather than for human thought and behavioural patterns in variable historical contexts.

Horton must have realized the fallacious implications of his arguments, because in three different rejoinders, two to Fisher and one to Ifeka-Moller's article, he virtually had to plod through the vast ethnography of African religions and the entire histories of the West African jihads in the vain attempt to find validation for his otherwise a-historical predictions.[13] The "most impressive" example he gave of the development of the cult of the Supreme Being in African Religions, "from which both Muslim and Christian influences were completely absent" was the development of the cult of the Supreme Being by the Aro people. The Aro were an Igbo clan who, acting as middle-men during the slave trade era, had developed a network of trade routes that cut across tribal boundaries. The Aro did indeed develop a more elaborate cult of the Supreme Being than was found in some other Igbo communities. However, it was not a monolatry (belief and worship of one God). Chukwu (the Supreme Being) through his oracle sustained and prescribed rituals to other local deities. It was therefore only an approximation to the monolatry of the converts to the missionary or Aladura churches. In the former case, the gods did not retreat. They were very much around and active with the support and approval of the Supreme Being.[14]

Similarly, Horton's attempts to link the jihads in West Africa to the expansion of trade and social change are not convincing. Monolatry and violent rejection of the deities by Christians and Muslims would be better understood if they were inspired by the long and uncompromising traditions of condemnation of polytheism in both world religions. The practice of adding one more deity to the list that makes up its pantheon is a characteristic feature of non-prophetic religions.[15] Forcing the gods to retreat is an innovation introduced by Christianity and Islam to Africa.

HISTORICAL APPROACH

Fisher wrote his article as a reaction to Horton's intellectualist interpretation of Islam in Africa. He argues that the history of Islam in Africa, covering a period of almost a millenium, displays a pattern of religious change which suggests that other explanations are necessary. His pattern is roughly characterized by three stages: quarantine, mixing , and reform. In the quarantine stage, the faith is represented by newcomers. Orthodoxy is relatively secure because there are no converts. As increasing numbers of local people embrace the faith, bringing with them elements of their traditional beliefs, a mixing stage ensues. Finally, after a lapse of decades or even centuries, a wave of reform sweeps away the mixing and restores the orthodoxy of the quarantine stage. The cycle may repeat itself.[16]

Fisher makes a very useful distinction between "conversion" and "adhesion". Conversion implies a "deliberate turning from indifference or from an earlier piety to another". While adhesion allows a believer to adopt new forms of worship as useful supplements to his former beliefs. The relative ease with which Islam in Africa can be adopted, encourages conversion as well as "mixing". Hence, he speaks of first and second conversions. The first is change of religious affiliation with or without orthodoxy. While the second is change from mixing to orthodoxy or fervency. Literacy in Africa has served not only as an effective means of preserving orthodox teachings, but also as "time bomb of reform". The reform movement may take the form of a jihad, or revivalism resulting in the reform of "mixed Islam". A jihad not only reforms "mixed Islam", but also makes new converts occasioned by the dissolution of traditional societies and the dislocation of traditional religion. Thus conquest has been a factor in conversion in Africa.

Fisher's brilliant historical analysis of conversion within Islam in Africa highlights the fact that conversion itself is a continuous process. There are many types of, and different stages in, religious change. There could be "adhesion" without conversion. While conversion itself could be a two step movement - "exchanging one faith (or none) for another, and exchanging indifference and dilution for fervency within the same faith. Each of these different kinds of religious change has their own motivations or causes. Fisher accuses Horton of concentrating on the first stage in conversion, with the result that "the essential underlying movement towards the second is lost".

However, it must be said that Fisher himself is guilty of a similar omission. He was so taken up with the second type of conversion that he forgot the first stage of conversion. How did local people come to adopt Islam in the first place?. Fisher does not say. And, this is in fact what Horton's article tries to explain. So, Fisher's arguments do not challenge Horton's main thesis. However, Fisher's analysis does underscore the importance of factors internal to the religion, to which conversion is made, in assessing "conversion". For Islam in Africa, according to Fisher, its contribution to conversion includes among other things its character as a prophetic religion, literacy, ritual prayers, pilgrimages, the fervour of clerics, and so forth. These serve the purpose of both keeping aglow the light of the faith during the mixing period, and at an opportune time, to precipitate a reform movement.[17]

DEPRIVATION THEORY - SOCIO-STRUCTURAL APPROACH

Ifeka-Moller's article is also a reaction to Horton's intellectualist explanation of religious change in Africa. She proposes as an alternative, a socio-structural explanation, which she claims better explains "conversion" understood as either "a change of affiliation from cult (traditional religion) to church, or from orthodox Christianity to spiritualist church (Aladura)".[18] Socio-structural factors, she argues, are the most fruitful field of research, rather than ideas and values which form the core of a belief system. "For if a cosmology is embedded in a social order, as were indigenous cosmologies in East Nigeria, and as Aladura belief is today, then we can only appreciate the extent to which ideas have shaped such new religious forms as Aladura churches if we focus on changes in the social order."

A good explanatory model, she continues, should account not only for cases of easy "conversions" but also for cases of resistance to conversion. Analysing the official census figures for eastern Nigeria for 1953, she identifies the Onitsha-Awka area of Igboland as a case of poor response to Christianity in spite of a strong exposure to missionary work, urbanization, and to social mobility within the Western imposed occupational hierarchy since the end of the 19th century. While Calabar and Owerri areas which have had comparatively less exposure to modernization during the same period, recorded "conversion" on a massive scale to Christianity and the Aladura churches.[19]

Factors which account for massive conversions in Owerri and Calabar areas include rapid social change, and a growing frustration among the inhabitants at the failure to reap the rewards promised by an acceptance of radical changes. They turned to Christianity which promised a new kind of power, identified with the power of the white man, which people could use to discover the secret of this technological superiority. Factors which encouraged a change to Aladura Christianity include frustration at the "exclusion from sources of secular power, scarce material resources and, hence, dependence upon alternative kinds of power, and the evident strength of old social forms and associated beliefs systems".[20] Secondary causes of conversion to Christianity mentioned by Ifeka-Moller include inter-denominational rivalry and education. Conversion to Aladura is also helped by "literacy and Bible knowledge".

The slow pace of conversion in Onitsha is explained by the fact that Onitsha had been opened up to Western values and modes of social differentiation over a period of two centuries which gave the people more time to adjust to modern commerce, literacy and Christianity. Besides, earlier contacts with Western civilization put them at an advantage over people from other areas in securing well-paid jobs during the colonial period. Colonialism did not bring to Onitsha any sudden disruption of traditional society, nor the frustration arising from unfulfilled expectation. The correlation between education and Christianity is not absolute, for whereas Onitsha has a high rate of literacy, it has a low rate of conversion.[21]

Ifeka-Moller's assumption that the high rate of conversion in the Calabar and Owerri areas is due to the deprivation suffered by these areas is, at best, a mere speculation. Even if one were to accept as premises in a syllogism the propositions that both deprivation and massive conversion existed in the two areas, one cannot validly draw the conclusion that deprivation was the cause of massive conversion. There is no evidence that converts see Christianity as an alternative to success in the modern world. Rather, it appears that they see it as a means to such a success. This would apply to both the deprived and to the better-placed people in society.

EVALUATION OF EXPLANATIONS OF CONVERSION

The above analysis has thrown up a number of important but ambiguous points, the clarification of which will, I hope, put into proper perspective the different explanations offered for the phenomenon of conversion. Firstly, the term "conversion" itself means different things to different authors. Because of this, authors often inadvertently talk at cross purposes. Secondly, the explanations do not bring out the distinction between "religious" and "non-religious" causal factors of "conversion". Where this is done generally there is a tendency to underplay the importance of the "religious" factors. Finally, none of the explanations argue the case for variable multicausal factors of conversion, which I think provides the most adequate explanation of the complex problem of conversion in Africa. I comment on each of these points.

The different senses in which the term "conversion" is used in the explanations range from mere change of membership (affiliation), to change of conviction. Change of affiliation could be from Traditional Religions to a mission church, or from a mission church to an independent African church, or even a lapse back to Traditional Religion. A change of affiliation does not necessarily involve a change in conviction. There might be what Nock called "adhesion", in which, "people stood with one foot on either side of the fence, adopting the new worships as useful supplements".[22] This must be distinguished from "conversion", properly so called and defined by Nock as the "deliberate turning from indifference or from an earlier form of piety to another, a turning which implies consciousness that a great change is involved, that the old was wrong and the new is right".[23] Thus the term "conversion" has been used to connote three different types of change:

i)   Change of affiliation without change of conviction - Adhesion, e.g. a "mixed" Islam or Christianity.

ii)   Change of affiliation with change of conviction - Conversion I, e.g. from Traditional Religion to fervent Islam or Christianity.

iii)   Change of conviction without change of affiliation - Conversion II, e.g. from "mixed" Islam or Christianity to fervency.

The counter accusations between Fisher and Horton show that scholars are not always agreed on which type of "conversion" is being explained. Thus while Fisher accused Horton of concentrating almost "exclusively on the first sense ... of conversion", Horton, in turn, accused him of concentrating on the third meaning while giving "no overall explanation of why the basic underlying progression has been towards a purer faith".[24] Some explanations tend to generalize from factors adapted for one type of "conversion" to the others. A brief look at the different explanations will put into perspective their understanding of conversion and the validity of the explanation offered for it.

Trimingham's view is that the disintegration, under the impact of modernization, of traditional societies and religions left Africans with no other choice than to embrace one of the three systems with universalist world-views - Islam, Christianity, or secularism. This suggests that the "conversion" he has in mind here is in fact adhesion. The African Independent churches are groups of converts who decamped from the mission churches because of the intolerant attitudes of these churches towards traditional beliefs. In this case we still have "adhesion". In other words, according to Trimingham, the vast numbers of Africans who drifted into the mission churches and those of them who decamped, were not converted in the types I and II senses but merely changed their religious affiliation. To describe Nock's categories, they hold "a middle ground in which religion develops in step with political advance and cultural exchange". This is usually an intermediate stage between "the system of religious observance of a small social unit with elementary needs and interests and no important contacts with other cultures", and the "religion of a prophetic movement in the first ardour of the founder". This is adhesion, not conversion. The factors which bring about such religious change are mainly socio-cultural - notably the collapse of the structures of the traditional societies. Islam or Christianity was adopted because these religions with their universalist outlook, happened to be there at "just the right time". One could, of course, say that the intolerance towards "mixing" attitudes which forced the Aladura to decamp, is a religious factor. However, the decamping does not represent a different kind of "conversion".

Horton's explanation is identical with that of Trimingham's, but has an additional point - that the drift into the mission churches was not simply a passive exercise. It involved some measure of rethinking and adaptation of traditional beliefs to the realities of the resultant socio-structural changes. He illustrated these adaptations by comparing the beliefs of the Aladura churches with those of traditional religion on the one hand, and with missionary Christianity on the other. With the mission churches they retain the belief in a morally concerned God, and a denial of the power of the lesser gods. With traditional religion, they retain the belief that divine power could be tapped and used for explanation, prediction and control of this-worldly events, or, as Horton would say, that the gods are both "theoretical entities and people".[25] Horton then concludes that the traditional African world-view, changed to fit the modern situation, would give identical results. Thus, Horton tries to show that there was in fact not only a change of affiliation but also a change of beliefs, but these are the natural responses of traditional cosmologies to socio-structural changes. It is thus still adhesion.

A possibility which Horton did not consider is that the leaders of the Aladura movement could have easily picked up these ideas from the Bible. Barrett has established a strong correlation between bible translation and Independency.[26] Founders of the Aladura churches are drawn mainly from the mission churches, and many were former evangelists in the mission churches.[27] Besides, as Horton himself admits, "Early Western Christianity also had a dual nature, its God, its Christ and its saints all being theoretical entities and people".[28] This is especially so with the Old Testament, which the Independent churches particularly treasure. In fact, the Aladura often refer to the discrepancy they see between missionary Christianity, which Horton called "Christianity of the Enlightenment", and the Bible, which this very Christianity claims as its source.[29]

Fisher's explanation is aimed at illustrating "the willingness and ability of Africans to make even rigorous Islam and Christianity their own".[30] His arguments therefore are aimed at demonstrating how converts in the "adhesion" stage, over time, develop a conviction about their faith. He thus concentrates on "conversion" types I and II, and thus does not confront Horton who spoke exclusively about adhesion.

Ifeka-Moller defines "conversion" thus: "I take conversion to mean a change of affiliation from cult to church, or from orthodox Christianity to spiritualist church". Her model is therefore adhesion and not conversion, which she explicitly excludes, "the extent to which a move ... is associated with changes of attitude and behaviour".[31]

RELIGIOUS AND SOCIO-CULTURAL FACTORS IN CONVERSION

Conversion as a socio-religious phenomenon has social as well as religious causes. Different authors tend to stress only one of these two causes and underplay the other, depending on their theoretical or faith assumptions. Of course, one could say that "ceteris paribus", the socio-cultural causes, or the religious causes come into prominence depending on the type of "conversion" one discusses, - on whether one is discussing mere "adhesion" or a change of beliefs and conviction, i.e. "conversion" types I and II. Most of the writers discussed have emphasized socio-cultural factors, apparently because they have interpreted conversion as mere adhesion, or as a change of religious affiliation. It is not unlikely that an author's religious persuasion also influences his or her choice of causes. Thus Evans-Pritchard has complained that "the great atheistic sociologists of religion have been fired with the conviction that, by establishing the causes (socio-cultural) of religious belief, they could thereby establish its falsity".[32] Horton has accused "committed Christian scholars", whom he described as "The Devout Opposition", of a reluctance "to provide an over all causal explanation". Of course, for him, causal explanations means a "socio-cultural" explanation. A religious explanation is not a cause. Conversion, he argues, must be shown to be "responses given by members of different socio-economic categories confronted with Islam (or Christianity) at a particular time or place".[33]

This is a perspective of Horton's approach which Gray felt most unhappy about. Horton's explanation, argues Gray, "would seem to overlook the possibility that the world religions may have introduced completely new concepts to the African religious repertory". "Missionary records", he continues, "show that the impact of Christian eschatology has had a profound effect on African cosmologies as well as on the imagination of individual Africans. This is further borne out by the vast number of millenarian movements, and by the reasons given by many Africans for embracing Christianity".[34] Professor Isichei agrees . The fervour of early converts was often linked with an overwhelmingly vivid eschatology, sometimes linked with visions and dreams.[35] The intense preoccupation of African Christians with eschatology reflects the absense of that dimension in traditional African religion. Barrett has stressed that the publication of the Scriptures in the vernacular is a crucial factor in the reasons for separatism.[36] Lamin Sanneh in a recent article has also stressed the role of the vernacular bible in the spread of Christianity and Independency, or as he put it, "the spirits of the ancestors, fitted with the engine of biblical revelation, transform local neighbourhoods into commuter belts of heaven".[37]

MULTI AND VARIABLE FACTORS OF CONVERSION

"Any thesis that claims to provide an over all causal explanation of a phenomenon as complex as conversion in Africa", says Gray, "is suspect".[38] A survey of the various explanations, if anything, shows that conversion in Africa is a multi-causal phenomenon. One needs only to take stock of the different factors mentioned by all the authors, to discover that an impressive list would emerge. Trimingham mentions the following factors: the crumbling of the structures of traditional religions, and the need for a universalist religion in place of the village religion. Horton mentions the rationalization of traditional beliefs in response to modernization. Fisher lists the following factors: literacy, conquest, migration, and the activities of devout clerics. Ifeka-Moller suggests: a desire for "White Power", deprivation, denominational rivalry, education, literacy and knowledge of the Bible. The list adds up to a total of twelve different factors. To these, one could add a host of others: inter-marriage, family and kinship ties, social prestige, patron-client relationships, and a desire not to be labelled as a "pagan" or as "primitive", as Christian and Muslim missionary propaganda called adherents of traditional religion.

Exposure to the Christian faith and Islam, and their missionary preaching and welfare programmes, are factors which are often underplayed in favour of supposedly underlying factors. The extent and depth of missionary influence in Africa has generally not been appreciated. The strength of a foreign Christian missionary presence in Africa has shown a spiral increase during the period of mass conversion. From two chaplains with the expedition to Sierra Leone in 1787, the total grew to over 10 000 missionaries in 1910, and to about 36 000 in 1970.[39] This is not including the even larger army of African ministers and catechists which has since joined them. Missionary enterprise and modernization often overlap. Missionaries had access to and in many cases controlled a large proportion of the instruments of social change: schools, welfare services, and the massmedia. One needs only to note that Islam has an even more formidable, if less modernized missionary force. No fair assessment of conversions in Africa can be made without listing Christian and Muslim enterprise as a major contributory factor.[40]

Conversions in Africa resulted from the encounter of the two major world religions, Islam and Christianity and westernization on the one hand, and different African cultures, social structures, world-views and economic systems on the other. The different approaches analysed above have generally not brought out the variable patterns of response to conversion in different regions and by different cultures in Africa, as this observation makes clear:

> The process of Christian conversion has varied from one part of Africa to another over the past 100 years; in some areas, such as Buganda (Uganda), entire populations accepted the new faith quickly; in others, such as most of the traditionally pastorist areas, there were only a handful of converts. In some areas, such as most of southern Africa, the chiefs were the first to be converted, in others, such as the Akan kingdoms of Ghana, they were the last; in some areas mainly women have become Christians, in others both sexes.[41]

This statement, if accepted, shatters the pretence of any mono-causal explanation.

Similarly, the reasons for the mushrooming of Independent churches in Africa are manifold. The intolerant attitude of many Christian missionaries towards traditional beliefs and practices was an important factor, but not the only one. The translation of the Bible, which provided "an independent standard of reference" to legitimize African grievances, was also a potent factor. In many cases independency was a protest against colonialism and the control exercised by foreign missionaries. Protestant missions spawned more separatist churches than Roman Catholic missions, while the preference by some African converts for pentecostalist forms of Christianity often resulted in a break with their non-pentecostal mission churches.[42]

CONCLUSION

Generally, one could say that the studies of conversion in Africa have been characterized by a number of tensions. First, there is the tension between views which explain African conversion as "old wine in new containers", and those who would see it as "new wine in old containers". The former view emphasizes that "African conversion" is no more than an adaptation or rationalization of traditional beliefs under the impulse of rapid social change, with the new religions having merely a catalyst role. The latter, on the other hand, perceives it as the outcome of a revolutionary effect of the new religions on the old ones. In other words, the former emphasizes "continuity" or survival of traditional beliefs, while the latter emphasizes "innovation" or the introduction of new elements. However, from an analysis of the above, it is clear that African conversion is both a process of the adaption of elements of traditional beliefs and the adoption of new beliefs. The dominance of the traditional or the new Christian or Muslim elements, may depend upon the various stages of conversion. Where there is only a change of affiliation, or "adhesion", the traditional elements may dominate beliefs. In conversion, proper, the change of conviction is in favour of the new faiths.

The second tension is between explanations which emphasize socio-cultural factors and those which emphasize religious factors. While both socio-cultural and religious factors are present at every stage of conversion, the religious factors tend to predominate at the stage of a change of conviction.

The shortcomings of all the explanations mainly derive from the ambitious attempts to provide a comprehensive explanation for an event as complex as conversion, in a setting as wide and diverse as the African continent. I have tried to suggest here, that a multi-causal rather than a mono-causal explanation has a greater chance of doing justice to such an enormous task.

NOTES

1. D.B. Barrett, *The African Independent Churches and their potential in Scripture Distribution* quoted by G.C. Oosthuizen, *Afro-Christian Religions, Iconography of Religion*, Leiden, 1979, p. 3. Whereas Oosthuizen gives 160 million as the population of Christians in Africa, The Cambridge Encyclopaedia of Africa puts both the Christian

26

and Muslim population in Africa at 100 million. C.f. *The Cambridge Encyclopaedia of Africa*, ed. by R. Oliver and M. Crowder, Cambridge University Press, 1981, p.1410 which puts the population of the Afro-Christian churches at between 5 and 10 %.

2. A. Oberti and L. Satori, eds., "La Salvezza Cristiana: La voce degli Episcopati dell'America Latina e dell'Africa al Sinodo dei vescovi 1974", *Quaderno ASAL 20*, Roma, 1975, p. 90. 7 million Africans become Christians every year, pp.99-100.

3. G.C. Oosthuizen, ibid. He calls these African Independent Churches Afro-Christian Churches. The same Churches have been called Independent Churches, Separatist Churches, Spiritist Churches.

4. J.S. Trimingham, *The Christian Church and Islam In West Africa*, SCM Press, London, 1955, p. 12-13.

5. J.S. Trimingham, *Islam In West Africa*, Oxford Clarendon Press, 1959, p. 21.

6. Ibid.

7. Robin Horton, "African Conversion", *Africa*, Vol. 41, No. 20, April 1971, c.f. *Aladura: A Religious Movement among the Yoruba*, London, 1968.

8. Robin Horton, Ibid., pp. 102-104.

9. Ibid.

10. M.J. Van Binsberg, *Religious Change in Zambia*, Paul Kegan, London, 1981, p. 20.

11. Humphrey J. Fisher, "Conversion Reconsidered: Some Historical Aspects of Religious Conversion in Black Africa", *Africa,* 1973, p. 27.

12. C. Ifeka-Moller, "White Power: Social-Structural Factors in Conversion to Christianity, Eastern Nigeria, 1921-1966", *Canadian Journal of African Studies*, Vol. 8, No. 1, 1974, pp. 55-72.

13. R.C. Horton, "On the Rationality of Conversion", Part I, *Africa*, Vol. 45, No. 3, 1975, p. 219, and Part II, *Africa*, Vol. 45, No. 4, 1975, p. 375.

14. C.f. W.B. Bakie, *Narrative of An Exploration Voyage up the River Kwora and Niger and Tsadda in 1854*, London, 1856, p. 313. C.f. also G.T. Basden, ed., *Niger Ibos*, 1966, p. 71.

15. A.D. Nock, *Conversion*, London, Paper Back ed., 1969. Nock's view of reaction of a microcosmic world-view to wide-scale socio-cultural change, sharply contrasts with Horton's position. Nock would accept that the scope of the world-view would be considerably expanded "in step with political advance and cultural exchange", by "adopting the new worships as useful suppliments" rather than "retiring the gods".

16. Humphrey Fisher, "Conversion Reconsidered: Some Historical Aspects of Religious Conversion in Black Africa", *Africa*, Vol. 43, No. I, 1973, pp. 27-39.

17. Ibid.

18. C. Ifeka-Moller, op. cit., pp. 55-72.

19. Ibid. 1953 census figures show that Christians in Onitsha constitute 26% of the total population of the area while Owerri and Calabar have 64% and 77% respectively. Horton objects to Ifeka's use of the census returns which lumps together Onitsha urban and surrounding rural districts.

20. Ibid.

21. Ibid.

22. A.D. Nock, quoted by H.J. Fisher, *Africa* , Vol. 43, No. I, 1973, p. 33.

23. Ibid.

24. R.C. Horton, *Africa*, Part II, Vol. 45, No. 4, p. 395.

25. R.C. Horton, *Africa*, Vol. 41, 1971, p. 96.

26. D.B. Barrett, "Church Growth and Independency as Organic Phenomenon, an Analysis of 2 000 African Tribes", *Christianity in Tropical Africa*, ed. C.G. Baeta, Oxford University Press, p. 269.
27. Akin Omayajowo, "The Aladura Churches in Nigeria since Independence", *Christianity in Independent Africa*, ed. Fashole-Luke, R. Gray, H. Hastings, and G. Tasie, Rex Collins, London, 1978, p. 96. C.f. also A. Kofi Opoku, "Changes within Christianity: The case of the Musama Disco Christo Church", *Christianity in Independent Africa*, p. 112.
28. R.W. Horton, "African Conversion", *Africa*, 1971, p. 96.
29. A. Kofi Opoku, op. cit., p. 109.
30. H.J. Fisher, op. cit., p. 27.
31. C. Ifeka Moller, op. cit., p. 51.
32. E. Evans-Pritchard, "Religion and the Anthropologists", *Essay in Social Anthropology*, London, 1962, p. 29.
33. R. C. Horton, "On the Rationality of Conversion", Part II, *Africa*, Vol. 45, 1975.
34. R. Gray, "Christianity and Religious Change in Africa", *The Church in a Changing Society*, proceedings of CIHEC Conference in Uppsala, 1977, pp. 349-350.
35. E. Isichei, "Encounter: Patterns of Perceptions of Christianity among Nigerian Communities over Time", *The Church in a Changing Society*, CIHEC - Conference Reports, Uppsala, 1977, p. 381.
36. D.B. Barrett, *Schism and Renewal in Africa: An Analysis of 6 000 Religious Movements*, London, 1968, p. 268.
37. Lamin Sanneh, "The Horizontal and the Vertical in Mission: An African Perspective", *International Bulletin of Missionary Research*, October 1983, p. 166.
38. R. Gray, ibid.
39. Elliot R. Kendall, "The Missionary Factor in Africa", *Christianity in Independent Africa*, p. 19.
40. J.S. Trimingham, *The Christian Church and Islam in West Africa*, 1955, p. 40
41. O. Roland and M. Crowder, eds., *The Cambridge Encyclopaedia of Africa*, Cambridge University Press, Cambridge, OUP, 1981, p. 409.
42. D.B. Barret, "Church Growth and Independency as Organic Phenomena: An Analysis of 2 000 African Tribes", *Christianity in Tropical Africa*, p. 219.

Religion, Development and African Christian Identity

Terence Ranger

INTRODUCTION

In the title I have been given by the organisers of this conference there are included three distinct notions - the notion of African Christianity, that of African identity and that of development. All three have been much debated but I find only one to be problematic. There have been many arguments in the past over whether this or that African church or sect is *really* Christian, just as there have been many arguments over whether any African who *is* really Christian can possibly share in an African identity. For the purpose of this paper, at any rate, I find it easy to short-circuit these arguments. I shall maintain that one of the great realities of twentieth-century Africa has been what Bengt Sundkler calls "the Christian Movement", a movement embracing churches of mission origin and churches of African prophetic provenance. I shall also maintain that *because* this Christian movement has been one of the great realities of twentieth century Africa it has also been, by definition, an aspect of African identity. All this seems to me to be straightforward, though I shall take some time to illustrate it.

What seems to me to be much more difficult is the notion of "development". It is notorious that development specialists disagree about how to define development, how to measure it and how to achieve it. Some emphasise that entrepreneurial enthusiasm is essential, others lay stress rather on egalitarian communalism. Some believe that a prosperous African peasantry has a key role in development, others that no development can be achieved until the peasantry is subdued and destroyed to make way for a rational large-scale agriculture which can support industrial expansion. Here I have my own prejudices and I shall state them straight away. I believe that development in Africa must be founded in the rural areas and that it must involve recognition of the hopes and ambitions of the peasant communities which constitute the vast majority of Africa's rural population. So I shall focus in this paper on the rural areas - just as missionaries and African prophets have always done. I shall argue, indeed, that in much of Africa a history of rural development, or underdevelopment, is inseparably linked with the history of the African Christian movement, through which so many peasants expressed their hopes and ambitions. Christianity in Africa has been essentially about rural change. Of course it has not been about rural change in any consistent direction. Peasants have used different types of Christianity for many different economic and social ends so that we need to understand the social history of rural Christianity in order to understand class differentiation in peasant societies as well as to understand the general history of agrarian change. Nevertheless, although Christian ideas have often been allied with aspirant rural capitalism, I shall argue in conclusion that the Christian movement in Africa, seen as a whole, has much more in common with the socialist transformation of peasant societies for which many African regimes are calling than those regimes or most Christian churches imagine.

I intend to demonstrate these propositions with reference to one particular case - that of Zimbabwe. I do this mainly and admittedly because I know the Zimbabwean case better than any other and have recently carried out research there on a range of topics related to the issues of this conference. But I also do it because Zimbabwe is an especially interesting case for us. It is a country in which the Christian Movement has become very significant indeed. It is also a country committed to socialist development, with a governing party about to define itself as Marxist-Leninist. It also has a vigorous private industrial and agricultural sector which the present government has done nothing to undercut. In Zimbabwe, therefore, debates about styles of development and about the interaction of state, capital and the churches have a particular liveliness and pertinence.

THE FUNDAMENTALLY COMMON CHARACTER OF MISSION AND
INDEPENDENT CHURCHES AS PARTS OF THE ZIMBABWEAN
CHRISTIAN MOVEMENT

Norman Etherington has recently complained that we possess very few studies of the social history of mission churches compared with the multitude of works available on African independent movements.[1] This has largely been, of course, because the independent churches are seen as so much more *African*. Historians interested in African opposition to colonialism have studied the independent churches as protest phenomena: African theologians, seeking to make their specific contribution to world theology, have sought for insights in independent church formulations and rituals: anthropologists, who have been almost always uneasy about the alien character of the mission churches and their de-culturing effect on African societies, have found in the independent churches fascinating evidence of African cultural resilience. When an anthropologist recently proclaimed the need for sociological studies of mission, what he meant was merely sociological studies of missionaries.[2]

Now, I wish to argue here that much of this has been misconceived. The independent churches are a fascinating and important object of study, of course, and I don't in the least wish to suggest that we stop being interested in them. But I do wish to suggest that it is time that social historians, anthropologists and even theologians became more interested in the inner history of the churches of mission provenance. And in particular I wish to suggest that we should see mission churches as much less alien and independent churches as much less "African" than has hitherto been the case. I see mission churches and independent churches as fundamentally similar in one respect: they are both first and foremost Christian movements which *await* Africanisation.

What do I mean by saying that we should see independent churches as "less African"? Clearly I don't mean anything very sweeping. I am coming on, after all, to argue that the whole Christian Movement must now be seen as an intrinsic part of African identity. But independent churches have been seen as drawing upon African religious traditions in a uniquely direct way and I think this is misleading. Churches which emphasise ecstatic possession by the spirit, which foster prophecy and spiritual healing and exorcism have been seen as continuations of African belief and practice. Yet these very features, which are taken as being most African, are in reality the most Christian aspect of such churches. They spring directly from increasingly strong tendencies in world Christianity in the late nineteenth and twentieth centuries. They spring in fact either from anti-establishment Christian Pentecostalism, as it developed in Europe and North America, or from evangelical revivalist tendencies within the major mission churches themselves. Few independent church leaders have claimed to be continuing African traditions. Most are anxious for their churches to be seen as part of a world movement; many claim legitimacy by means of a connection with one or other of the Euro-American movements of prophecy and healing. It is, of course, true that this type of theology and practice has enabled intense interactions with African societies but as I have already said, these inter-actions are not "natural" or given but have to be worked for and worked out. In saying all this I am saying no more than Sundkler and Hollenweger have already shown for South Africa.[3] But I can illustrate the point by carrying their work north across the Limpopo and looking for a moment at the relationship between world Christian traditions and African independ-ency in Zimbabwe. In Zimbabwe it was not until the second half of the 1920s and the 1930s that there was any significant growth of African "spirit" churches. When these did take off, it is true that the Zionist move-ments of the 1920s arose because labour migrants had made contact with entirely black-led churches in South Africa, and that the various Vapostori churches of the 1930s arose as entirely indigenous movements of prophetic inspiration and commission. Yet the whole development can only be understood against a background of the long diffusion of pentecostal and revivalist ideas in Zimbabwe. This diffusion had taken two forms - the direct operation within Zimbabwe of pentecostal missions and the expression within the Protestant mission churches of enthusiastic movements of revival.

By the 1920s the ideas which were to animate the African independent churches in Southern Rhodesia had long been expressed there by healing and pentecostal missions. And the alarm and suspicion which the Rhodesian administration was later to show towards the African churches had long been displayed towards white pentecostalists. Earliest of these was the South African General Mission which in 1897 established itself in Gazaland in eastern Zimbabwe. In 1915 the SAGM station at Rusitu was the scene of an astonishing movement of enthusiasm. This followed on the arrival there of Rees Howells, product of the great Welsh Revival and a noted healer. Howells found that the missonaries already at Rusitu "had been studying the subject of the Lord's Second Coming" so that "there was already preparation of heart for a work of the Holy Spirit".

The people had already heard that Mr and Mrs Howells came from the land where the Revival had been, and straightaway asked them if they had brought that blessing with them. Mr Howells told them that the Source of all revival is the Holy Ghost and that He could do among them what He had done in Wales. They had no word in their language for revival, so he told them about Pentecost: that it was God who had come down then, moving upon the hearts of men and women, and had swept multitudes into the Kingdom; and that He would do the same with them, if they were willing to repent.

Within "six weeks the Spirit began to move upon the Christians of Rusitu", falling first on a dozen of them as they prayed for revival in Howell's house.

Howells "recognised a sound he had heard in the Welsh Revival". On the following Sunday the Spirit descended:

> As I preached in the morning (wrote Howells) you could feel the Spirit coming on the congregation. In the evening down He came ... He came upon a young girl, Kufase by name, who had fasted for three days under conviction that she was not ready for the Lord's coming. As she prayed she broke down crying, and within five minutes the whole congregation were on their faces crying to God. Like lightening and thunder the power came down. I had never seen this even in the Welsh Revival.

Soon there was "praying in every kraal"; there were "two revival meetings every day for fifteen months, without a single break"; "hundreds were converted but we were looking for more - for the ten thousand upon whom He had told us we had a claim".

Here, in a district which later experienced movements of independent African religious enthusiasm, was all the atmosphere of those subsequent pentecosts. And in 1919 with the influenza epidemic Howells responded just as the African Apostolic churches were later to do:

> The Lord reminded Mr Howells how, in the intercession for sick people in the village at home, he had been led to challenge death a number of times. Would he be able to challenge it again here on a much larger scale?

"The heathen" came to Rusitu, blaming the epidemic on Christian converts - it was "a curse from the ancestral spirits", angry at breaches of custom. Howells confronted them with serene assurance: however many deaths there might be in the kraals, Rusitu was under divine protection:

> The Holy Spirit said to His servant: "Tell them that no-one can die on the station". So he answered, "No! Not one will die on the mission station ..." I knew that the Holy Ghost was stronger than death.

No-one on the station did die, so the story continues, and eventually chiefs and people from miles round came into the station for protection - "if you come, you must admit that our God is the living God, and that He can help where the witch doctors and the ancestral spirits have failed". Even the most "gospel-hardened" found that "the Holy Spirit was stronger than the flu". Soon new converts were carrying the message deep into Portuguese East Africa, where they were promptly arrested by the authorities.[4]

Next on the scene, this time in Matabeleland, was the Apostolic Faith Mission. In May 1916 26 converts from Southern Rhodesia came for baptisms at the AFM's station in the Zoutspanberg, "full of the Spirit, speaking in tongues":

> I do not know what particular fancy branch of religion this is (wrote the Native Commissioner, Gwanda, Matabeleland, in September 1916, as the AFM spread in his district), but it appears to combine the Rollers, Tumblers, Groaners, etc. [5]

In the years that followed young white Afrikaners carried the Apostolic Faith message into Midlands, Mashonaland and Manicaland, preaching "the new-old religion" to receptive congregations: the Chief Native Commissioner reported the AFM as "an entirely new sect whose doctrines ... among other things, inculcate faith-healing" and so "put wrong ideas into the native mind".[6] The influence of the Apostolic Faith Mission waxed and waned but it was strongly reviving at the end of the 1920s and in the early 1930s. It was impossible for the administration, indeed, to distinguish between the processes which were bringing thousands of adherents to the AFM and those simultaneous processes which were giving rise to the indigenous Apostolic churches of Johana Masowe and Johana Maranke. Both mission and African movements won converts, thought the Native Department, with "the same uncanny behaviour".[7]

In the 1920s there also arrived the Pentecostal Mission and the Full Gospel Church, which were influential in some of the Reserves near Salisbury. And in 1923 "the people of an American Swedish Sect, Pentecost people or Philadelphians", set up their Swedish Rhodesian Mission in Matabeleland.[8] It can be seen therefore that many of the ideas and practices which it is often assumed originated with the independent Zionists and Apostolics arose out of an ambience created by pentecostal missionary activity.

But some of these ideas had found expression within the more orthodox mission churches as well. On 19 December 1926 the old Swedish missionary, Hans Nilson - the patron in Gwanda both of the Swedish Rhodesian Mission and of the Apostolic Faith Mission - wrote to complain of the prohibitions that the administration sought to place upon pentecostal mission work:

> As to the haste of baptism (wrote Nilson) they acted in accordance with the Scripture, as in the Acts of the Apostles people were baptised the same day they confessed or accepted the faith.

African converts to the AFM could not understand government hostility. It was all very well to talk of the demarcation of spheres between church and state, but while "we can sell our oxen ... we cannot sell or hand over 'Amakolwa', Christians, without their own wish or consent". In any case, he concluded, the established missions might complain, but "Weslyans forty years ago they were very much like this missions today. In fact I have said they are the images of Weslyans".[9]

In fact some missionaries of the Wesleyan tradition were still not all that different even in the 1920s. The American Methodist Episcopal Church, which had established its influence over precisely those areas of Manicaland which were later to be the seed-bed of the African Apostolic churches, firmly believed in Revival and the Pentecostal experience. The manifestations of this American Methodist enthusiasm struck other missions and the administration as dangerous. In July 1918 African evangelists of the AmMEC experienced a Pentecost at Old Umtali - an event to which African members of the church now look back as signalling its true rooting in Africa.[10] The manifestation of the Holy Spirit in Umtali alarmed Anglican and administrator alike:

I am told they are all very excited (wrote Robert Baker of the Community of the Resurrection) ... Excitement of this kind, if uncontrolled, is sometimes serious.

Revivalist meetings are being held by the American Methodist Mission (wrote the Native Commissioner, Umtali) for the benefit of their native adherents and it is sincerely to be hoped that the result will be beneficial. The inherent spiritualist tendency of the native mind readily responds to the mystification of religious ritual, and I consider that great care and discretion should be exercised in awakening, not what is felt by the preacher, viz., religious fervour, but the abandonment of the native who considers himself to be under a spiritualist influence over which he has not control ... The American Methodist native teachers here (he wrote two months later) have been preaching the second coming and the natives are wildly excited. Most of the young men have taken to preaching ... Down here some of the natives have been wildly excited.[11]

For some years after the 1918 revival the American Methodists were not allowed to open any more schools or stations.

But this did not dampen the revival fervour in the church. In the early 1930s church women had their own revival and thereafter came to dominate the annual camp meetings, where the Holy Spirit descended, healings were performed, witchcraft charms were burnt, and evil spirits were exorcised. To Anglicans there seemed little difference between these camp meetings and the gathering of the African independent Vapostori. Indeed, I wrote in 1980 a paper which argued that Johana Masowe's Vapostori movement sprang out of the American Methodist context of his home village.[12]

Even the Dutch Reformed Church, which we customarily think of as so stern and unbending, possessed its own traditions of revival.[13] In 1929 "the evangelical mission of Dr. Scheepers" produced manifestations of enthusiasm in the Victoria province of southern Zimbabwe which neither the church nor the administration could distinguish from independent Zionism.

Indeed, Reverend Louw, writing from Morgenstern mission, did his best to blame any excesses of DRC revivalism on Zionist machinations:

> I regret that there was some excitement amongst a number of Natives after the evangelical mission ... Natives are, as you know, very emotional and given to gross exaggeration ... I wonder in how far the so-called "Church of Zion" movement are responsible for the disturbance. They are most emotional in their methods, fall on the ground, profess to be moved by the Spirit, under whose influence they receive obscure messages.[14]

It was as difficult for Louw as it has been for most commentators on the intrinsically "African" character of Zionist belief and practice to accept that at moments there was not all that much difference between Dutch Reformed Church members and Zionists.

I don't of course mean that the African Zionist and Apostolic churches of Zimbabwe were no more than continuations of a Euro-American counter-establishment tradition. In their hands that tradition engaged deeply with the problems of African societies. But in engaging with those problems the leaders of the spirit churches saw themselves above all as representing a Christianity that was totally hostile to African tradition. And if the independent churches were much less traditionally "African" than we have often supposed, the mission churches were much more so than we often recognise. I believe that the conventional picture of missionary history is profoundly misleading. We normally imagine that the early missionaries, possessed by an ethnocentric confidence in their own culture, imposed a rigid European structure of belief and practice on their converts, and that this gradually gave way to looser and more enlightened attempts at "adaptation" and ultimately devolution of control to Africans. In fact my own recent research on the three major mission churches of eastern Zimbabwe has led me to construct a very different sequence. In the early period - no matter what may have been the prejudices and incomprehensions of the missionaries - several factors allowed for a very great deal of African agency and the emergence of a much modified practice. It was in this period that a popular Christianity was founded. Later, as the bureaucratic structures of the churches were built up and as African teachers and clergy emerged from professional training schools, there was an attempt to impose an orthodoxy of manuals and service-books. This gave rise to tensions and sometimes led in itself to the breakaway of independent churches. But in the churches I have studied many African Christians had already laid hold of, laid claim to, what had become a local ecclesiastical tradition. The churches had become theirs, to be defended against independency by means of African-led revival movements within the mission denominations and against over-rigorous clergy by the maintenance of an underground practice of popular Christianity.

This emergence of a popular Christianity in eastern Zimbabwe depended on three chief factors. One was that however culturally arrogant the early missionaries were, they did take pains to try to seize the local landscape and to create new centres of spiritual power. In a paper which I am writing simultaneously with this one, I explore the care with which Anglicans created Christian cemetries as focal points of the new religion; the imagination with which they built up patterns first of district and then of national pilgrimage. I also explore the way in which Catholics took hold of every dominant feature of the local terrain with shrines and perambulations, and how the American Methodists developed the "holy ground" of the sites at which their annual camp meetings were held and at which the Holy Spirit came down. Finally, I seek to show how these new patterns of mystical geography were taken hold of, further elaborated and exploited for their own ends by African Anglicans, Catholics and Methodists.[15] Often the early missionaries, who helped create these symbolic continuities with and transformations of the old spiritual landscape, are today remebered along with African pioneers as healing and miracle-working founders of an indigenous church.

The second factor was the well-known dependence of early missionaries upon their African agents. The report of the committee on evangelisation to the American Methodist Umtali District Conference in January 1911 sets this out very plainly:

In nearly every case (converts) have been brought to Christ thru the influence of Christian natives. Many times the Christian Community with its higher and better standard of living seems to have appealed to (them). These Christian men and women command the utmost respect of the heathen people. It is giving them an example of the ripe fruit of Christianity at this stage of their development. I believe that a group of such Christian laymen, who live the normal Christian life, who of course preach also, but depend upon manual labour for their living, make a mighty strong evangelising agent ... The boys I have talked with very frequently mention some native preacher who seems to have helped them very much. The boys have very seldom said that they have been helped by white missionaries. I suppose these spiritual matters require the close heart to heart talks that are more likely to occur between two natives than between a native and a white man. Further it is not possible for the few white workers that we have to reach any large number of people personally. But there is also a considerable number who profess Christianity in the isolated kraals thru the preaching of boys who have been to the mines or to schools.[16]

Both the Methodists and the Anglicans in eastern Zimbabwe first extended their influence in eastern Zimbabwe by bestowing their recognition on local men who had set up as teachers and preachers on their own accord:

> The natives in this district have a craze for learning reading and writing (reported the Native Commissioner, Umtali in 1909) not confined to the younger people only - old women, wives and mothers, may be seen daily struggling over almost indecipherable characters scrawled on a slate by some native who has had a better chance than they.[17]
>
> Many natives gather together (wrote the Superintendent of Natives, Umtali, in 1912) a few of their compatriots and regularly instruct them in the rudiments of reading.[18]

Typical of these enterprising founders of local Christianity was Nehemiah Machakare, a returned labour migrant, who set up his own church and school in 1907 at Muziti in Chiduku Reserve in the Makoni district, Manicaland, which later became the headquarters of American Methodist Episcopal activity in the whole area:

> I started to preach the Gospel among the villages (in) 1907 (Nehemiah told his new American Methodist colleagues later). I was preach the Gospel in kraals there I been born. I was thinking to build the Church of God, then I build the small hut. Then I saw the people came so many. I pray to God to give me powers to carry the poles to this house ... And God bless us in that day repenteth 48 people, women and girls and boys. Now God give me helpers to carry the poles. I build the large church ... Then I hold the 4 services every Sunday there came great congregations every Sunday sometimes 112 and 124 ... Then I have visited among the kraals ... to spread the Gospel among the heathen and preach pray day times and night times. I thank my God has been with me where I preach the Gospel among my friends. It is made my heart glad to me when I see my friend received the Gospel.[19]

Nor do we have to rely on Nehemiah's own claims. In 1916 one of his Muziti converts described how he had become a Christian:

> I was live at Muziti kraal but was do many heathen things ... Nehemiah he did come to Muziti kraal ... I did saw Nehemiah. He was begin to preach and he did come to my house. He said to me please you pray God because God is our Father in heaven but I did not answer. But he said to me, do you about seed, if you plant they not died. This time I did repent. It was 1909. But Nehemiah he was a great preacher.[20]

The great Anglican diffusion through Manicaland was similarly based on men of this kind, the founders of new Christian villages, over which they presided with apostolic power:[21]

> These stations have grown out of and are part of the native communal life (wrote Canon Edgar Lloyd in 1915) ... The teacher, or leader, of such a station lives under the same conditions as ordinary natives and has the same communal rights.[22]

In 1929 - when young, professionally trained teachers were crowding in and threatening to displace the founders of this rural Anglicanism - Lloyd wrote a retrospective eulogy of the way in which they had rooted a rural popular Christianity:

> This village work is extremely important ... because it has to be done by themselves ... (The out-station) is really a Christian community centre ... It is wonderful to see in heathen Africa the religious devotion of so many villagers and the real influence the Christian religion has on their lives ... The particular work undertaken by this Mission (is) that of preaching Christ in the villages and in the country schools of the villages. Africa is a country of villages: of cultivated patches, often hand-tilled, of herds of small cattle, of wood fires in huts and long nights of discussion ... To hold the villages for Christ is to hold Africa that now is.

The men who held the villages for Christ, the founder-evangelists, were men of character, but alas lacking learning, perhaps men not so dissimilar from certain of those first disciples and apostles denominated "unlearned and ignorant men".[23]

Here in these first teachers and preachers two strands of popular Christianity came together. The teachers themselves represented a group of amibitious young "progressives", able to break away from chiefs and elders and establish their own villages. And they gave their congregations the benefit of their spiritual power:

> Here is Benjamin Katsidzira preaching at Chipfatsura out-station during the Revival of 1918: a boy lying on the rock outside the church, mocking the church-goers and surrounded by drinking companions, was struck dead: "The drunkards tried to wake him up by lifting, but they failed to remove him from the rock. He had become attached to the rock by an unknown power ... Those who were in the Church were praying to God so that they could receive the Holy Spirit". Then the Spirit descended and they processed out of church. As they came to the rock, Abraham Tsoka took the boy's hand and said "In Jesus Name, stand up and go to the Church". Straightaway the boy sprang up ... This miraculous healing spread from lip to lip. The drunkards threw away their calabashes of beer for fear that they would become stuck to them for life - and it was just as well for them, if this oral account can be trusted:
>
> As they were all here at the Church ... singing the very same song ... Ponomono, miraculously, as he was smoking in the Church, stood up and flew to a tree outside like an arrow and was seen sitting between two branches. Still another result of the Revival was the submitting of charms to the Church. Two boys who had their charms which they believed would turn them into lions if they wished to, stood up and gave their testimonies ... They presented all their charms to the congregation and were converted to Christ the very day.[24]

Once these punishments and miracles had taken place in any congregation, the teachers and evangelists retained power. In 1923, for instance, the Native Commissioner, Umtali, intercepted a report from the main American Methodist mission village in Makoni district, Gandanzara. In 1918 the Holy Spirit had come down on Gandanzara and the surrounding hills had each been made sacred, the main one coming to be thought of as the local Mount Zion, from which the new law had been proclaimed: thereafter the Gandanzara congregation regularly received miracles:

> God does things for his people who know him in their hearts and if they are in trouble they depend on God (went the report from Gandanzara). Now in the year 1922 we have great trouble at the village of Gandanzara, with hunger and great heat, it did not rain for a long time, it rained at other places but not here ... The heathen came to Philip, son of Gandanzara, and said: "Allow us to be given spirits that the rain comes, behold we die of hunger" ... All the people laughed and said: "All the people of Gandanzara are dying of hunger". All the people of the church continually prayed to God until God heard the prayers of His people. Then it rained hard, and the gardens of the people have good crops. The people thank God greatly for his kindness.[25]

The African AmMEC minister at Gandanzara in the mid 1930s, Reverend Silas Kasambira was a famous rain-maker who could also bestow through prayer the gift of pregnancy to infertile women.[26]

I could go on for a long time happily citing these testimonies to the popular character of Manicaland Christianity, but the point, I think, is made. It remains to bring out the third factor, which I shall elaborate upon later. More was at issue in the spread of Christianity than the creation of appealing symbols and rites, than the effusion of Christian spiritual power, than the ambitions of the founders of Christian villages. Africans seized upon Christian symbols and powers and upon Christian literacy because these had practical utility in relating to the colonial economy. The 1911 American Methodist report on evangelisation, which I have already cited, goes on:

> A question I have worried about very much is whether the people are not more attracted by such things as learning, improved dress, food and standards of living than by the Gospel itself. Often the boys and girls have said that they wanted to go preaching in crowds. They say: "when we stand up to sing they will see that we look different from them and our faces are different and they will say: 'We want to be like that'".[27]

The Anglican Canon Hallward expressed similar reservations about the "conversion of a district - practically of the people", a movement "obviously of God; we can do and have done extraordinarily little":[28]

> I find it very difficult (wrote Hallward) to know how far the teachers are spiritual men with a love of souls. They are far more efficient than might be expected in managing

their unwieldy schools ... and they do somehow manage to get into them a capacity to read the Bible, a little elementary writing and a fairly sound knowledge of the rudiments of Christianity. That people come to their schools, and attend regularly for the most part, is due to the general desire for the New Learning more than to any attractive power of the teacher, or, one must add, to the desire for the Gospel. There is a general movement that carries people along, and they accept all that it implies, clothes, slates, reading, catechism and the Ten Commandments. But whether the teachers are actuated by real missionary motives or not; and whether or not those who come to learn start as a rule with anything beyond a vague desire for progress; at any rate the results are wonderful ... A teacher is quite aware of the dignity of his office; and he is treated with marked respect ... Dare we trust the ministry in their hands? Dare we keep the work in our own?[29]

In fact Hallward was posing here a series of false antitheses. It is clear that men like Nehemiah were "spiritual men with a love of souls" and also "quite aware of the dignity of his office" and also possessed by a "desire for progress". The mission churches rooted themselves in eastern Zimbabwe in a rich mix of pilgrimage and progress, rain-making and reading, healing and hygiene. Gandanzara, the village ringed by hills made sacred by the Holy Spirit, with its rain-making and fertility-giving ministers, was also the stronghold of entrepreneurial plough agriculture in Manicaland, with the highest rate of literacy. In 1975 a Methodist elder from Gandanzara wrote to the District Commissioner urging that headman Philip Gandanzara be succeeded by another firm Christian:

The late headman was a Christian. His influence did spread to the village that we were all brought up under church ... His village became a centre of civilisation and attraction which made it easier for the missionaries to contact other districts, making his village an example of what the District Commissioners wanted to produce.[30]

THE CHRISTIAN MOVEMENT AS PART OF AFRICAN IDENTITY

I have tried to show that many African members of both independent and mission churches have come to define themselves primarily as Christians - or equally as Christians and Zimbabweans. But I have also tried to show that both mission churches and independent churches introduced into African societies ideas and practices that originated outside Africa. Does that mean that African Christian self-identification clashes in some way with a more rigorous definition of "African identity"? I think not. To begin with both missionary and independent Christianity awaited Africanisation: some aspects of both were never "Africanised" but the greater part of both *has* been "Africanised", not in the sense of being absorbed into some metaphysical "traditional" culture, but in the sense of being taken up by Africans and used by them in order to survive or prosper in modern African society. In this matter I agree with Paulin Hountondji and his polemic against the advocates of Negritude or African Personality. Admittedly Hountondji's concern is to legitimate more secular aspects of so-called "Western" thought but his contentions apply equally to the African Christian Movement:

> We speak of African civilization as "traditional" in contrast to Western civilization, as if there could be African civilization, Western civilization, in the singular, and as if civilization were not, by nature, a permanent clash of contradictory cultural forms ... European civilisation is not a closed system of values but a set of irreducible cultural products which have appeared on the European continent; or, at a deeper level, it is the set of these products and of the creative tensions which underlie them ... in the forms they have assumed in the past and in the as yet unpredictable forms they will assume tomorrow ... Nor is African civilization a closed system in which we may imprison ourselves (or allow ourselves to be imprisoned). It is the unfinished history of a similar contradictory debate as it has proceeded, and will continue to proceed, in that fraction of the world called Africa...
>
> When we use the more vivid phrase "traditional African civilization", we add a value connotation, and pre-colonial civilization as a whole is being contrasted with so-called "modern" civilization (that is to say, colonial and post-colonial civilization, with the connotation "highly Westernized"), as if they were two essentially distinct systems of values ... We ignore, or pretend to ignore, the fact that African traditions are no more homogenous than those of any other continent, that cultural traditions are always a complex heritage, contradictory and heterogenous, an open set of options, some of which will be actualized by any given generation, which by adopting one sacrifices all the others. We ignore, or pretend to ignore, the fact that cultural traditions can remain alive only if they are exploited anew ... Above all, we ignore or pretend to ignore the fact that African cultural traditions are not closed, that they did not stop when colonization started but embrace colonial and post-colonial cultural life. So-called modern Africa is just as "traditional" as pre-colonial Africa in the only acceptable sense of the word "traditional" - tradition does not exclude but necessarily implies a system of discontinuities.
>
> What we must recognise today is that pluralism does not come to any society from outside but is inherent in every society. The alleged acculturation, the alleged "encounter" of African civilization with European civilization, is really just another mutation produced from within African civilizations ... The decisive encounter is not between Africa as a whole and Europe as a whole: it is the continuing encounter between Africa and itself.[31]

AFRICAN CHRISTIANITY AND AFRICAN DEVELOPMENT

If we borrow some phrases from Hountondji we can say that the future development of Africa will be the fruit of a "contradictory debate", the outcome of "the decisive encounter ... between Africa and itself". In this encounter it is tempting to see African Christianity as being on one side as against some other manifestation of "modern" African identity, such as African Marxism. I don't see it in this way. In a country like Zimbabwe, Christianity has become "Africanised" by being used in so many different ways that a debate about development has been and is being conducted within Zimbabwean Christianity itself. Moreover, it is not too much to say that if the Zimbabwean government is to have any chance of success in involving the peasantry in a socialist transformation it will have to understand the history and trajectory of the rural Christian movement.

I shall very rapidly sketch some of this history now. I shall begin with the various mission churches and their resultant popular Christianities already discussed in this paper, namely the popular American Methodism, the popular Anglicanism and the popular Catholicism of eastern Zimbabwe. Each of these rural popular Christianities has its own economic history; each came to correlate with a particular kind of peasant involvement with the colonial economy. This happened as the result of an interaction between the teaching of each church about society with the particular opportunities and choices of rural communities. Thus the American Methodists sent out evangelists almost everywhere in Manicaland but strong centres of popular Methodism built up where rural entrepreneurs had good access to markets for agricultural produce. Similarly, Anglican centres developed largely among smaller-scale peasant producers with an ethic of egalitarian village communities. The core Catholic centres tended to be in areas more remote from communications and markets, where most men had to leave for wage employment, leaving their wives to undertake a subsistence cultivation. The ideology and ritual of the three churches fitted these varying peasantries - American Methodism providing in its combination of strong discipline, intense emotional experience and "the gospel of the plough", an ideal mix for entrepreneurial pioneers; Anglicanism providing an explicit ideology of village communalism; and Catholicism offering both a sacralisation of place which brought back labour migrants from all over southern Africa on pilgrimages home and also a paternal discipline over resident female cultivators.

Certainly I found these correlations to be true for Makoni district. American Methodist missionaries aimed at economic transformation:

Poverty is the word that perhaps best describes the lives of these people (wrote O'Farrell). Poverty of material comforts; poverty of social ideals; poverty of religious conceptions. Richness must be poured into their lives ... to bring regeneration to the entire economic, social and spiritual life.[32]

They believed that traditional religion imposed fear-ridden prohibitions on agri-cultural enterprise and that Christian conversion would liberate economically as well as spiritually. At the end of an American Methodist pamphlet recounting the experiences of three African converts was added:

To the African this fear and superstition is most real and he orders his life accordingly. No advance can be made socially or economically until he is spiritually converted and delivered from such domination. Economic betterment cannot take place until fear and superstition are removed from agriculture and health ... The Church is seeking to make the abundant life in Christ available for all, through spiritual transformation, social reformation and economic betterment.[33]

The key convert in this respect was Abraham Kawadza, whose career we can see through the eyes respectively of the missionary evangeliser, the missionary agriculturalist and subsequent admiring African oral testimony:

Kawadza was a naked, low type of African (wrote E B Caldwell in 1920), filled with superstition and fear of the white man ... He lived his life in nakedness and shiftlessness, as most natives do, content to live on whatever of a living his two wives were able to make for him ... He does not look as though he had enough sense to come in out of the rain. The missionary was not at all enthusiastic over the thought of taking such material into his church .... (But) as soon as he became a Christian he began to try to cover his nakedness ... He began to desire better methods of farming than the hoe, and he borrowed a plough from one of the missionaries and got a span of oxen and began to plough and plant and it seemed as though every time he put seed into the ground God blessed it. He built large huts to hold his grain and stored it. Then he began to buy stock and in a little while was by far the wealthiest native for many miles around.[34]

The missionary agriculturalist recalled Kawadza's own agrarian and ideological initiatives:

Kawadza came to me many times asking such questions as: Would the grain grow in his fields the same as it does for the missionary? Would any harm come to him or his family if he used a plough instead of using beer to call the neighbours to help do the digging? Would the rain come the same on his fields? For him it was a real serious matter, for this was the first plough to be purchased by a native in Rhodesia. The rain did fall on Kawadza's fields for his first crop was about four hundred bushels of corn instead of the usual fifteen or twenty.[35]

African testimonies about Kawadza stressed his pre-colonial prestige - he had fought for chief Mutasa in his wars and with his father raided enemies in Mozambique. In the eyes of African Methodist converts he was very far from a "low type of African". But African testimonies also stressed Kawadza's new wealth:

> Abraham Kawadza was one of the richest men of that time. He had a lot of property. To give but a few examples, he had cows, goats, sheep, horses and waggons ... He had a lot of oxen and used to travel on horse-back ... He used to go to town on horse-back to go and order his things for his business ... Though he had many workers he could not allow them to go for work before they had a prayer ... Since he had a lot of cows he fed his workers on milk and meat ... He would bring (his mother and grandmother) to church in one of his carts.[36]

It became prestigious within the church to claim conversion at the hands of Kawadza, who ended up as one of the mere handful of Africans to purchase a farm in the white commercial area.

In Makoni district there were numbers of little Kawadzas. Gandanzara village became the "demonstration" congregation, close as it was to the Umtali market:

> The success of our native people in agriculture (wrote the mission agriculturalist in 1932) is really wonderful ... At present there are hundreds of ploughs owned by natives and the crops grown are really wonderful. Some of our best stations like Gandanzara where the new methods of agriculture have taken a firm grip are a wonderful demonstration. At this particular station every person who has any cattle has a plough and there are forty-three ploughs owned by the people there. These people who own the ploughs are no longer poverty stricken. They are the foundation of progress in the village.[37]

And in addition to whole villages converted to Methodist entrepreneurialism, there were new settlements of two or three men devoted to increased pro-duction. Thus Bishop Abel Muzorewa's father was a pastor-teacher for the American Methodists. In the early 1930s he decided to "try his hand at farming" and together with two other ex-pastor-teachers he settled at Chinyadza in Chiduku Reserve, Makoni, where he "discovered some forty to fifty acres of relatively rich soil" and opened up "rich green fields of maize, groundnuts, rapoko and beans". "Released from pressures to con-form with past ways", the three Methodist families flourished. Their wagons carried scores of sacks of maize to the line of rail. Their children were launched on an educational career which was eventually to carry one of them to his brief prime ministership.[38]

Makoni Anglicanism had a different atmosphere. Canon Edgar Lloyd was a spokesman for the village ministry - "Our Blessed Lord lived for nearly the whole of His life ... in the little village of Nazareth", a second generation of Anglican teachers were told. "Let us then think it is a great honour to work for Christ in a little village and to work for our own people, and to live the life of our own people".[39] On leave in England Lloyd took a course in "Peasant Pottery" at the Camberwell School of Arts and Crafts; his wife, Elaine, took a weaving course at the Peasants Art Guild. Back in Makoni they sought to make each Anglican village a centre of relevant craft production. The Lloyds did not aim to foster Kawadza-style capitalist farmers. Instead they backed the Anglican pioneer teachers, who presided over communities of small-scale producers; annual pilgrimages brought marching columns of peasants, carrying their totemic banners, from the scattered out-stations to Lloyd's church at St Faith's. And everywhere that Lloyd went in his ceaseless itinerations of Anglican territory, he met peasants carrying their crops to market, the surplus of their "cultivated patches, hand-tilled". The Resident Commissioner who toured the Anglican zone of south Chiduku Reserve in 1920, reported strongly against the proposal that African peasantries should be evicted from the land and that it be given over to whites. The whole territory was dotted with a network of Anglican villages, he reported, each:

> in charge of a native teacher. These men are married, are well educated, and of more than usual intelligence. At each station there is a well built church ... It was also evident that some attempt was being made to keep the native kraals ... clean and tidy. The men and women were better dressed than is usually the case in kraals so far removed from centres of European occupation. [40]

These mild modernisations were beyond the reach of popular Catholicism in Makoni district. The Catholic core area came to be the mission farm at Triashill and St Barbara's, on the eastern edge of the district, a rocky and remote area, cut off from markets. Until the 1960s, when a motor road was opened up and fertilisers offered some chance of a marketable surplus, the Catholic missionaries paid relatively little attention to agriculture. They concentrated instead of building an exclusive and coherent folk Catholic community. The missionaries brought in the Ultramontanist peasant cults of nineteenth century Europe - the Lourdes grotto, miracle-working statues of Our Lady of Fatima, pilgrimages to every hill on the mission land, thus sacralising the land and bringing the migrant labouring men back home. Priests exorcised locusts - driving them off in a Protestant direction, blessed seeds, prayed for rain. The main contribution made by the Catholic missionaries to "modernisation" was their provision of education, possession of which gave their young men an advantage in the southern African labour market.

Now, of course, all these missions came to develop their school system greatly and all of them have come to provide educated men and women who are now filling professional and bureaucratic posts in independent Zimbabwe. The careers of such people have blurred the outlines of the older correlations between popular Christianities and economic status. Still, there have been recent surveys carried out which suggest that the economic and social pattern of early folk Christianity is sustained to this day. In February 1982 Dr Michael Bourdillon presented a talk to a conference on "Emerging Christianity" on the topic of "Christianity and Wealth in Rural Communities in Zimbabwe". Reviewing the work of Martin Daneel, of Mary Aquina Weinrich and of Roy Theisen in the 1970s, he suggested that some correlations between economic status and Christian denomination persisted. Broadly, churches of an evangelical Protestant character seemed to produce members "significantly more orientated to social and economic development than their neighbours"; Anglicans came somewhere in the middle; "Catholics were only slightly more wealthy than traditionalists". "The economic successes of Reformed Church members stood out precisely in contrast with members of the Roman Catholic Church".[41]

The one change of pattern is in itself a significant one. Prophetic African churches arose in Makoni during the 1930s, at least partly as a protest against the collapse of the colonial economy in the Depression. The Vapostori of Johana Masowe or Johana Maranke argued that mission education had proved pointless, that mission church demands for church dues were oppressive, and that Africans should contract out of a colonial economic system which could suddenly deprive them of wage employment or of markets for their crops:

> Baba Johan had the conviction (says Amon Nengomasha) that one could not lead a proper and holy life unless he could fend for himself. This is the most important belief expressed by Baba Johan. If he satisfied his material needs, he would be able to satisfy his spiritual. It was very difficult at first because most of his converts lived in rural areas and knew only about agriculture. The first message to these people was, "first of all, you people must learn to work together. Have a common field". [42]

Later Johana Masowe led many of his followers out of the rural areas and they became self-employed artisans - shoe-makers, basket-makers, etc - on the outskirts of southern Africa's towns.

Now, there is no doubt that in its early years the Apostolic movement expressed a reaction against the entrepreneurial ethic of American

Methodism. Yet the Vapostori were even more resolutely hostile to traditional religion than were the American Methodists, and they were just as much characterised by those qualities of rigour, proscription, committment to the life of the church, internal cohesion which Theisen has held to explain the economic success of Reformed Protestantism. It is not surprising, then, that many Apostles are now conspicuous for their enterprise and prosperity. Bourdillon remarks that a good deal of data shows "a correlation between the independent churches and successful agricultural production"; summarising Angela Cheater's work on Vapostori African Purchase Areas, he comments that "the Vapostori provided an ethic which had a clear economic advantage; this advantage was recognised by church members; nevertheless, the expressed motives for attending services and the organisation of the church were based on religious rather than economic issues".[43] No doubt the same is true of Vapostori artisans, but none the less their significance in contemporary Zimbabwe is striking. The June 1984 issue of *Moto* comments on the implications of government policies of craft apprenticeships and compulsory education for the Vapostori:

> If education in fact ... means educating youth away from productive work in the rural areas, then another very serious mistake will be made if all children are compelled to attend school up to the age of sixteen. If this proposal becomes law, what will it do to the Vapostori. In many areas they *are* the informal sector. They are the only tinsmiths, carpenters, welders, basket-makers in some rural centres, and they provide most of these services in many places. But their community is built on, among other things, a rejection of formal education and of formal employment, and this is what makes them such valuable self-employed craftsmen. It may no longer be true that one never sees an unemployed muPostori, but they are still much rarer than among any other group of people one can identify. Forcing formal education on them would either push them into conflict with the government or imbue their children with the unrealistic aspirations that all will find comfortable white-collar jobs afterwards. Either way, a community which makes a very real and productive contribution to the rural economy would be destroyed. They might be wrong on other matters, like refusing hospital treatment for their children, but on this point it must be admitted that they have proved themselves right, and we would all be a lot worse off without them.[44]

RELIGIOUS TRADITIONS AND THE GUERRILLA WAR

In Makoni district, as elsewhere, these various traditions of popular Christianity and their associated histories of economic development went through the fire of the guerrilla war. In a forthcoming book [45] I have described what happened in some detail. Here I will summarise very briefly.

American Methodism became a hostage to its bishop, Abel Muzorewa; American Methodists backed his African National Council with all the enthusiasm of the frustrated entrepreneur, but many of them remained with Muzorewa right through the period of the Internal Settlement and found themselves an object of attack by ZANLA guerrillas. Methodist entrepreneurial enthusiasm is at something of a discount in Makoni at the moment, though it remains to be seen whether it will not be able to take advantage of whatever rural economic opportunities develop. At the other end of the spectrum, Makoni folk Catholicism collaborated completely with the guerrillas. Triashill and St Barbara's became the nearest thing to "liberated areas" in the district; the guerrillas accepted folk Catholicism as the local ideology and worked closely with the Irish priests. Although they have been the least engaged in agricultural change in the past, there is much speculation today about the self-help potentialities of locally based Catholic communities, who sustained themselves during the war in isolation from the urban superstructures of the church.[46] In the middle, as always, Makoni Anglicanism was divided into the two distinct traditions of its past: the original Lloydian tradition of rural communalism flowed into the agricultural co-operative experiments of St Faith's and Makute, which some see as the foundations for communal production on a much larger scale today; the dogmatic, bureaucratic traditions of the church, which were imposed on rural Anglicanism in the 1930s, continued in the 1970s to issue pronouncements which alienated guerrillas and their peasant allies. The guerrillas were baffled by the Vapostori, who seemed to be fore-runners in repudiating white authority but who also held an ideology of pacificist abstention. The whole process was a complex and confusing one and it leaves no-one very clear about which of these Christian traditions is the most relevant to development today. I could end by seeking to choose myself between Methodist entrepreneurship; Catholic radical self-help; Anglican co-operativism; Apostolic self-reliance. Instead I want to consider this Christian movement as a whole in its relationship to the announced aspirations of the Zimbabwe government.

AFRICAN CHRISTIANITY AND RURAL SOCIALISM IN ZIMBABWE

Since independence there has been much debate about the relationship of Christianity to Zimbabwean Socialism. A fascinating body of Zimbabwean Christians has emerged under the name of Buriro/Esizeni - the Shona and

Ndebele words respectively for "threshing floor", an appropriately rural image:

This threshing floor for ideas was set up shortly after Zimbabwe won its independence (the first issue of the Buriro/Esizeni bulletin tells us), by a group of concerned Christians from different church denominations. It had become clear that there was a yawning gap between the preaching of the gospel and the worship and structural life of the church on the one hand, and the religio-cultural and political realities of the people on the other hand. It was also found that outside of formal church programmes the people of Zimbabwe were reflecting critically on the meaning of their Christian faith in the context of liberation war, the developing national socialist character, and their traditional roots. Buriro/Esizeni seeks to encourage and bring out into the open this reflection by providing both oral and written opportunities for people to express freely their experience and to plan together their development accordingly. It is our hope that through these efforts the church of Zimbabwe may become a "church of the soil", rooted in the example of Jesus Christ who became human in order that the gospel might be relevant to all of human experience.[47]

From their first publications Buriro/Esizeni has campaigned against Western analytical theology and in favour of African experiential theology; against formal ecclesiastical structures and for local communal initiatives. The notes on their first seminar in September 1981 emphasise that "under the colonial regime the development of critical thinking was discouraged" and that what was needed now was "group action for the promotion of the masses". "The concept of the pastor/priest/religious leader as the expert on things spiritual and thereby as unchallengeable was seen as particularly detrimental to the development by the people of their own theology."[48]

In July 1982 Buriro/Esizeni confidently asserted that:

Methods and ideas which were effective in previous years no longer had the same impact since the liberation war had changed congregations from unquestioning passive recipients of the word coming from authority, into challenging, analytical thinkers who recognize that degree of authority which is within themselves.[49]

Buriro/Esizeni sought to set up "work-cells" or to revive the *pungwes* which during the war had been the meeting places of the ideas of the guerrillas and those of the peasants. They commented the "unique approach" of one Protestant pastor:

newly appointed to a church that had been the brunt of much resentment and physical abuse during the war. He spent some time visiting the people and helping them with reconstruction work at their homes. Eventually he summoned people to "morare" (morale-building through dancing and singing songs of liberation and encouragement) in the ruined church building. By the second week, the people wanted to dialogue with him, in the manner developed during the war between the freedom fighters and the community members ... They dialogued on the presence of God in their field work, reconstruction, illness and achievements. After some weeks of this, the people had worked out their own form of worship.[50]

In its issue of June/July 1983 the Buriro/Esizeni bulletin carried an enthusiastic review of a book by President Canaan Banana, *Theology of Promise. The Dynamics of Self Reliance* . And indeed Banana's book is the fullest expression of a Zimbabwean theology of liberation. Banana launches a violent assault on what he depicts as the typical Christian religiosity of the colonial period. It was, he says, paternalistic and fatally spiritual, in the sense that it made a total division between the spiritual and the material life. It thereby inculcated an ideology of the impoverished, fatalist, dependent, focussed on individual survival rather than collective self-help. Christian peasants, in Banana's unsparing view, were ready to change from one Church or party to another depending upon which offered the better opportunities; had little sense of duty to society; had little "understanding of society as a collective enterprise"; left aid to the poor to the state or the church as external bodies; vented their anger on those closest to them rather than on those responsible for their poverty. During the war admittedly, peasants collaborated with guerillas in a way which showed their potential for development. "But the potential of our peasants could not be developed fully during the war ... and the work started then should be continued now with greater vigour and intensity".

Banana hopes that the churches can take their part in such work. But to do this, he says, they have to transcend their past. They have to preach a new gospel, in which there is no disjunction between spirit and matter, in which love has to be expressed in power to transform:

There is no division between power and love ... If power is repudiated on moral or religious grounds, how can the poor defend themselves? Can there be any greater love than to lay down one's life at the hands of the rich in the process of changing society? Can we not say that there is no love without politics? ... One of the failures of many a Christian leader in the past has been to attempt this work of liberation by continous reference to the gospel, and by admonishing people to take Christ's example. They were unaware of the laws regulating socio-economic relationships ... The liberating aspects of the gospel became obscured and in many circles the churches have been regarded as a cover-up for exploitation. In order to educate the masses ideologically much more than preaching is needed ... Change only takes place when past and present experiences are compared with future perspectives and everything makes sense. This change takes place in a group ... Christianity is essentially a revolutionary struggle which brings out of man all the potential that the creator is expecting from every one of us ... For years we have been lamenting (poverty). We have been very compassionate indeed and, as "good" Christians we have been helping the poor with alms.

For the church of Zimbabwe today the revolutionary changes and effectivness of our government and of the people of Zimbabwe in solving their problems single handed should be an eye-opener ... The Lord has spoken to us once more as he spoke to the people of olden times in their liberation ... Only a genuine form of Christianity which springs from the people's experience will find room in Zimbabwe ... The people of Zimbabwe are ready to express their faith in their own terms: to know who God is ... A theology from the people means that the people are living the historical experience of their liberation and experience that event in new socio-economic structures ... The poor and oppressed are emerging from their culture of silence to speak to a world that has long tried to deny their existence.[51]

All this is splendid. Yet I cannot help but wonder whether Banana - and Buriro/-Esizeni - are not seeing it too much as something totally new, something which stands in stark contrast to the previous history of the Christian movement in Zimbabwe. What strikes me most about Banana's book is that he is not so much calling for a first "theology of the people" to emerge in Zimbabwe: rather he is calling for a development for the 1980s *similar to* the early seizure of Christianity by Zimbabweans in the first decades of the twentieth century. Banana writes:

It is impossible to plan and construct the future without the materials already available. In Zimbabwe ... in the social order (this principle) takes cognisance of patterns of thought and behaviour deeply ingrained in the minds of peasants and workers. It is impossible to create new patterns of thought different from the very minds of the people ... We are not talking about ignorance here, but about those relationships ... resulting from historical developments ... They are not necessarily negative but they can be viewed as attempts at local solutions in the constant struggle for survival.

But from this admirable proposition he goes on to sketch out the passive culture of mere survival which I have already summarised. I would argue that the material I have already presented in this paper shows that in taking account of the "patterns of thought" of the peasantry one has to reckon with a popular Christianity which was indeed an "attempt at a local solution".

Moreover, I would argue that most of the things for which Banana indicts colonial Christianity were not true of this popular Christianity. Thus, as we have seen, it was certainly not true that popular Christianity made a distinction too sharply between the spiritual and the material - early missionaries were uneasy at what they saw as the over-materialistic character of popular Christianity. Again, both Buriro/Esizeni and Banana are anxious for a locally grounded theology, springing out of the needs of the community:

> The experience of the local community is the new burning bush (writes Banana), burning with the intensity of the continual every day struggle for a better life, for meaningful social liberation, for the total liberation of the poor.

But was not the experience of the local community the "burning bush" of early Zimbabwean rural Christianity? Did not the self-founding Christian villages of eastern Zimbabwe burn "with the intensity of the continual every day struggle for a better life"? Indeed, I am conscious as I explore the character of that early popular Christianity that its vital units are the local village communities - the missionaries play something of the role of the co-ordinators and providers of resources which Buriro/Esizeni sees the Zimbabwean government playing today in its relations with local self-help "basic communities". Admittedly there was later a freezing over period in which the ecclesiastical establishment bore down heavily on local initiatives - just as one has all too much reason to fear that in days to come the Zimbabwean state establishment may bear down too heavily on local self-development groups. But it nevertheless seems important that Zimbabwean Christians should recall that their religion once allowed them to be initiators of willed socio-economic change and that it can allow them to be so again

Plainly Banana wishes to back certain types of popular Christian rural change rather than others; equally plainly he wants to enlarge the consciousness and reinterpret the old desire for power. Throughout Banana's book runs a constant reference to Christs reply to the disciples of John. The old popular Christianity gave the same answer as Christ himself:

> Go your way and tell ... what things you have seen and heard; how that the blind see, the lame walk, the lepers are cleansed, the deaf hear, the dead are raised, to the poor the gospel is preached.

It was *this* legitimating claim which the 1918 revival allowed the African teachers and evangelists of the American Methodist Episcopal Church to make, or which the prophetic commission of Johana Masowe allowed his Apostles to make, or instrumental Catholicism allowed African Catholic leaders to make. This deep desire for *power to remedy*, so intrinsic to Zimbabwean popular Christianity, has recently led a white missiological scholar to deny that it really is Christianity at all. [52]

Now Banana suggests a different answer in the new Zimbabwe:

> When messengers come from the western countries asking about the experience of liberation, the gospel is re-enacted and the words of Jesus can be heard again. The first question asked is the same as that asked by the messengers of John: Is this the salvation that you were expecting or are we to await another one?

Incidentally the messengers from overseas arrived in the same day that children all over the country returned to school after the holidays to start a new school year ... Primary school education became free all over the country. Free medical services were provided for 80% of the population and minimum wages established ... The messengers were given the following answer:

Go back and tell your masters in Europe and the United States what you have seen and heard: land is given to the peasants so that they can plough and obtain their food from the earth; the sick are looked after and the ignorant are educated; co-operatives are formed so that people work together and can produce more for the whole country; those who were in prison before are now helping the people in reconstructing the new society; the hungry are filled with good things and the rich sent away empty. Happy are those who do not lose faith in God when they see his work among his people.

The Theology of Promise is nothing else than to see how the promises of God are being realised every day and his presence among man made evident. [53]

This seems to me to be an answer fully in the tradition of Zimbabwean popular Christianity - *provided that* the local rural Christian community really *can* see with its own eyes that enough land is being provided and that the hungry really are being filled and the rich really are being sent away empty-handed. It is not in fact quite like that yet in rural Zimbabwe, so if this enlarged popular Christianity is to become a reality the local communities have to be shown what they can do to achieve these "promises of God". So far as I can see, though, much more of the groundwork for an assertive peasant "theology of promise" exists and has historical roots than President Banana or Buriro/Esizeni allow for. Maybe the structures of state and church should worry less about rural political education and worry more about acting at the centre so as to provide a context in which rural Christian self-help can flourish without defeat and disillusionment.

NOTES

1. Norman Etherington, "Missionaries and the Intellectual History of Africa: A Historical Survey", *Itinerario*, 2, 1983, pp. 116-143. In a comment relevant to the subject of this paper Etherington remarks that "nothing so clearly fixes the present peripheral status of African missions as a subject for historical research as their almost total neglect by the scholars of under-development, dependency and political economy who have dominated so many other aspects of African studies during the last decade".

2. T.O. Beidelman, *Colonial Evangelism: a socio-historical study of an East African mission at the grass-roots*, Bloomington, 1982.

3. W.J. Hollenweger, *The Pentecostals*, London, 1972, pp. 111-175; Bengt Sundkler, *Zulu Zion*, Uppsala, 1976, Chapter 1.

4. Norman Grubb, *Rees Howells. Intercessor. The Welsh Coal Miner a Prince with God*, Christian Literature Crusade, Pennsylvania, 1952, Chapter 24.

5. "The Native Work of the Apostolic Faith Mission of South Africa. Report No. 1, July 1916"; Native Commissioner, Gwanda to Superintendent of Natives, Bulawayo, 26 September 1916, file N 3/5/1/3, National Archives, Harare.

6. Chief Native Commissioner to Acting Administrator, 20 November 1919, file A 3/6/8, NAZ.

7. For the history of the Apostolic Faith Mission see files A 3/6/8; N 3/5/1/3 and 4; S.84/A/275; S.138.17, 1924 to 1925 and 1925 to 1928; S.1542.M8, 1937 to 1938; S.1542.M8B, volumes 1 and 2; S.1542.P10, 1934 to 1936, NAZ.

8. For Swedish pentecostals in Southern Rhodesia see file N 3/5/1/7, NAZ.

9. Hans Nilson to Chief Native Commissioner, 19 December 1926, file S.138.17, 1925 to 1928, NAZ.

10. In the Old Umtali mission archives are collected dozens of oral reminiscences from African pioneers of the American Methodist church, both male and female. These collections were made by Shepherd Machuma and they constantly dwell on the legitimating experience of the 1918 revival.

11. R.H. Baker to Superintendent of Natives, Umtali, 10 September 1918; Native Commissioner, Umtali, report, July 1918; Native Commissioner, Umtali to Native Commissioner, Mrewa, 27 September 1918, file N 3/5/1/5, NAZ.

12. Terence Ranger, "Poverty and Prophetism. Religious Movements in the Makoni District, 1929 to 1940", University of Zimbabwe, Henderson Seminar, No. 51, April 1981.

13. Gerdien Verstraelen-Gilhuis, *From Dutch Reformed Mission Church to Reformed Church in Zambia*, Franeker, 1982.

14. A.A. Louw to Chief Native Commissioner, 26 December 1929, file S.138.17, 1928 to 1931, NAZ.

15. Terence Ranger, "The uses and abuses of the concept of popular religion: pilgrimages and holy places in twentieth century Zimbabwe", forthcoming in *Past and Present*.

16. T.A.O. Farrell, "Evangelisation", 18-19 January 1911, green file, "Early District Conference", Old Umtali Archives.

17. Native Commissioner, Umtali to Chief Native Commissioner, 6 October 1909, file NUA 2/1/8, NAZ.

18. Superintendent of Natives, Umtali to Chief Native Commissioner, 8 May 1912, file NUA 2/1/10, NAZ.

19. "The Report of Nehemil Machayire", 1908, Green file "Early District Conference", Old Umtali Archives.

20. "Testimony of Paul C", Testimonies collected in 1916 from teacher trainees at Old Umtali, Old Umtali Archives.

21. Thus in December 1902 Archdeacon Upcher reported a delegation from a kraal where "a young native ... who was once a servant to one of the clergy at Salisbury ... has taught and prayed ... Now they ask for a teacher". In August 1910 Edgar Lloyd, touring out-stations in Chiduku Reserve, Makoni district, wrote: "It is very wonderful ... how these schools are springing up. This particular work has sprung from the initiative of a man who is 'yet but a catechumen' He got them together, caused them to build their Church school and taught daily in the school what little he knew ... On Sunday he

would march his flock over to St David's, some seven miles away". In August 1911 Lloyd described how Jacob at Tandi "began work there on his own initiative (he lives there) and worked as a teacher for a year without pay". Because of drunkenness, he had moved his house and church half a mile away from the chief's village; "later on it is probable that a Christian village will grow up around him".

For an account of an early African Anglican pioneer see "The Life of Benjamin Mutseriwa and his work at St Faith's". Patricia Chater collection, file K, NAZ. Trekking around the out-stations in 1914 is described as "a long story, suffering and struggle. With assess and tents for 8 weeks they went east and west and south and north, through the forest ways where the wild things grazed. During the day it was the birds that entertained them and at night their hearts thumped as they heard the clatter of hooves and the roaring of lions".

22. Edgar Lloyd to Native Commissioner, Makoni, 19 October 1915, file N 3/5/1/3, NAZ.
23. SPG Annual Reports, 1929, USPG Archives, Westminster.
24. "Gwawawa (Chipfatsura)", Machuma file, "Out-stations", Old Umtali Archives.
25. Report from Gandanzara, Daniel Chipenderu, 7 January 1923, file NUA 3/1/1, NAZ.
26. "Life History of Reverend Silas Pambayi Kasambira", Machuma file "Persons", Old Umtali Archives.
27. T.A.O. Farrell, "Evangelisation", 18-19 January 1911, green file, "Early District Conference", Old Umtali Archives.
28. These expressions about the Christianisation of Manicaland are those of Canon Etheridge, writing in September 1909. White missionaries, he wrote, merely go round, "speak a few words of encouragement and pass on, more and more conscious of the barrier which separates white from black. And yet the thing is being done".
29. Canon Hallward, St Augustine's, Ascension Eve, 1914, *Mashonaland Quarterly Paper,* Vol. 89, August 1914, p. 9.
30. T. Gwatidzo to District Commissioner, Makoni, 10 August 1975, file "Gandanzara. Headman", District Commissioner's office, Rusape.
31. Paulin Hountondji, *African Philosophy. Myth and Reality ,* London, 1983, pp. 160-162.
32. T.A.O. Farrell. "Report", *Journal of the Rhodesian Annual Conference,* 1926, p. 28
33. E.L. Sells, *What Three 'Twice Born Men' of Africa Have to say concerning their Experiences,* n.d., p. 3.
34. E.B. Caldwell, "When Savage Africa goes on Evangelistic Trail", green file, "Sells Letters" Old Umtali Archives.
35. G.A. Roberts draft, green file, "E.L. Sells", Old Umtali Archives.
36. "Abraham Kawadza", Machuma file, "People", Old Umtali Archives.
37. G.A. Roberts, "Report", *Journal of the Rhodesian Annual Conference,* 1923, p. 67.
38. Abel Muzorewa, *Rise Up and Walk,* London, 1978.
39. St Faith's Pastor-Teacher Handbook, 1935, file ANG 16/1/10, NAZ.
40. High Commissioner to Administrator, 4 March 1920, file A 3/18/39/10, NAZ.
41. M.F.C. Bourdillon, "Christianity and Wealth in Rural Communities in Zimbabwe", revised version of a paper presented to the conference on Emerging Christianity in Modern Africa, Cumberland Lodge, Windsor Great Park, February 1982.
42. Interview with Amon Nengomasha, 17 February and 3 March 1977, AOH/4, NAZ.
43. Bourdillon, *op. cit.,* p. 19.
44. "Rural craftsmen face extinction", *Moto,* 24, June 1984, p. 15.

45. Terence Ranger, *Peasant Consciousness and Guerrilla War in Zimbabwe: A Comparative Study*, London, 1984.

46. Ian Linden, *The Catholic Church and the Struggle for Zimbabwe*, London, 1980; J. Kerkhofs, *The Church in Zimbabwe. The Trauma of Cutting Apron Strings*, Pro Mundi Vita Dossiers, January 1982.

47. "Greetings to our readers", *Buriro/Esizeni/Threshing Floor*, Vol. 1, No. 1, April 1983.

48. "Notes from the Seminar on African Culture, Christianity and Socialism", Harare, 26-27 September 1981, p. 1.

49. "Projects Investigation Report", July 1982, p. 2.

50. *Ibid.*, p. 3.

51. Canaan Banana, *Theology of Promise. The Dynamics of Self Reliance*, Harare, 1982, pp. 43, 50, 106, 107.

52. H. Bucher, *Spirits and Power. An Analysis of Shona Cosmology*, Cape Town, 1980.

53. Banana. *op. cit.*, pp. 119-120.

Religion and Politics in Zimbabwe

Ambrose M Moyo

THE RELIGIOUS SCENE IN ZIMBABWE

Religion has always occupied a central position in the life, thought, and institutions of most African peoples. The history, societies, and the nature of the African peoples cannot properly be understood if separated from their religious beliefs and practices. Before the dawn of the modern era with its gravitational pull towards secularization, African peoples in general were known to be extremely religious. This is still true for the majority of them. Atheism is foreign to the African soil.

The people of Zimbabwe are no exception. Religion in Zimbabwe manifests itself in various forms. There are, firstly, the traditional religions which share a common faith in the existence of a Supreme Being who is believed to be the Creator and Sustainer of the universe. He is known by as many personal names as are the tribes inhabiting the country. Among the Shona, who constitute the majority, His personal name is *Mwari*. This name is derived from the suffix *mu* and the verb *-ari* which means "to be". When put together *mu-ari* would mean "He who is". The term expresses the fact that the Supreme Being *is*, and there can be no fitting name for Him other than the one which acknowledges that *HE IS*. There is obviously a striking resemblence with the "I AM" (Jahweh) of the Old Testament.[1] Nevertheless, for the Shona people of Zimbabwe this Supreme Being is believed to be the source of all being. His praise names, which are descriptive of His nature and functions, include the following:

Musiki	-the Creator
Muvumbipasi	-the moulder of the earth
Musikavanhu	-the creator of man
Nyadenga	-the owner of the heavens

Samasimba	-the owner of all power and authority
Mutangikugara	-the eternal one (literary the first to be)
Dzivaguru	-the huge pool
Chidizivachepo	-the little pool that never dries up
Chirazamauya	-the giver of blessings
Chirozvamauya	-the one who can withhold blessings

In addition to these praise names, which describe various aspects of the peoples' faith in Him, He is also believed to be all wise (Muzivi wazvose), to be a righteous and a just God, and to have a special concern for orphans and widows. He is indeed a transcendent Being who is at the same time immanent.

My research on Shona traditional religion has confirmed the existence of a tradition that speaks of the Shona people having originated at a place called Guruuswa, which is believed to be somewhere north of the Zambezi River. Our interest in this tradition lies in its claim that the Shona fathers were called, through a voice that spoke to them through trees, grass or other natural phenomena, to leave Guruuswa and journey to some promised land. As they travelled south they were guided by the same voice (izwi), which they believed to be the voice of Mwari Himself. Food was miraculously provided, the sick were miraculously healed, and they were guided in directions free from hostile nations. Upon arrival in the promised land, the various clans were each allocated their own piece of land, and that Voice chose as its place of residence Great Zimbabwe. The Voice later moved from there to a place then called *Runji Rusingatungwi Nguvo,* which today is known as Matongeni. This is now viewed by Zimbabweans as the holy shrine of Mwari. There the Voice continues to be consulted on national, and today even on personal, matters. In times of drought and other national calamities, delegations are sent to Matongeni from all over the country. Even individual politicians or their wives are known to have visited Matongeni. After independence big national ceremonies have been organized there to ask for rain and to give thanks for the attainment of independence. It must be mentioned that at Matongeni there is a resident priesthood to attend to all religious matters pertaining to the holy shrine.

It is apparent from the above description that as far as the Shona people are concerned, God is not the "remote High God" assigned to them by some early missionaries and anthropologists.[2] One might also add that the traditionalist when faced with some grave and serious danger, such as finding oneself face to face with some devouring beast, could appeal directly to Mwari for help. The Shona people generally attribute lightning and thunder to Mwari, and when there is a storm people appeal directly to Mwari in their fright. There is an awareness of the presence or nearness of Mwari which cannot be adequately explained by the influence of Christianity or Islam. The Shona language is full of expressions and proverbs which express this consciousness.

Nevertheless, under normal circumstances people communicate with Mwari through their ancestor spirits (*vadzimu*). These are believed to function as intermediaries as well as spirit guardians. African peoples in general have very high respect for elders. If there is something important to be communicated one has to go through an intermediary. As an example, if one is to approach a prospective father-in-law for permission to marry his daughter, one has to go through a marriage broker (*munyai* or *samukuru* in Shona). Likewise, to approach a chief one has to go through a sub-chief. It is therefore quite natural in African thought that God, being the greatest and most powerful of all the elders, namely those that are alive and the "living dead", should be accorded the highest form of respect. It is believed, therefore, that the ancestor spirits are the most fitting mediators between God and man, and between man and God. My informants, most of whom were grandparents and spirit mediums, emphasized that the *vadzimu* are not worshipped. Where this has become so it is the result of human sin which closes people's eyes to the distinction between God and his creation. Nevertheless, in certain matters ancestor spirits are believed to have authority to act independently, hence they can get angry and demand that they be appeased. They are, however, believed to be ultimately responsible to God. God rules and sustains the universe through them, hence they must be obeyed. Very often delegations to the Voice at Matongeni, are told that the problems encountered by their communities are due to lack of respect for the *vadzimu*, especially by the young generation. Some of my informants argued that God and the *vadzimu* are one, that they work together, and that the *vadzimu* are ministers of God. Hence when God is offended, so are the *vadzimu* and the reverse is also true. God can inflict punishment through the ancestors. By appeasing the ancestors people believe they are also appeasing God. Others have said that by worshipping the ancestors they are in actual fact worshipping God.

Other ethnic groups in Zimbabwe have the same basic beliefs as the Shona. They have different names for God as they speak different languages. In Ndebele the Supreme Being is called *uNukulunkulu* (the Great great one), *uMdali* (the Creator), *uSomandhla* (the Almighty). He is worshipped through the ancestor spirits (*amandlozi*). The Sotho call Him Modimo and he is worshipped through the *badimo* (ancestor spirits).

African traditional religions continue to exert tremendous influence over the majority of the people of Zimbabwe. Even those who have become Christians have continued their ties with traditional religions. During the colonial era African religions and cultures were heavily suppressed by both the missionaries and the colonial administrators. Schools were used as platforms from which to proselytize and to destroy the African cultures and the peoples' identity. The result was that many nominal conversions to Christianity occurred, but those same people practiced their traditional beliefs underground. Independence resulted in a revival, or resurfacing, of African traditional religions. One can safely say that the majority of the people of Zimbabwe practices some form of traditional religion, or a combination of traditional religion and Christianity.

The second dominant and perhaps the most influential of all the religious traditions found in Zimbabwe is Christianity. It is estimated that between 50 and 60% of the population are Christians, although quite a large number of them also belong to the camp of African traditionalists. Christian missions were only able to establish Churches towards the end of the nineteenth century. Unfortunately there was too close a relationship between the missionaries and the colonial settlers, so much so that until very late they supported colonial policies. In colonial Rhodesia, agriculture (under the Land Aportionment Act of 1931 or the Land Tenure Act of 1969), the manufacturing and mining sectors, and even social services such as education and health, were, as R.G. Mugabe has observed, "so organized as to enhance the worth of the white bourgeoisie and diminish the social status of the African".[3] Where was the Church when all this was happening? What was its attitude? Let me quote again from Mugabe as he sees it:

> Christianity for years acquiesced in the policies of successive regimes that, contrary to its morality, impoverished the majority in favour of the minority, although in the fulfilment of its religious role it built Churches for the evangelization of those it saw being impoverished by capitalism, schools for the limited education for some of their children and hospitals for their limited health care. The Church then dared not stand in opposition to the state and condemn its inhumanity to the black majority population until the most violent and final face of colonialism was reached when it became jolted by two factors, firstly the bitter criticism it received from African nationalism, and secondly, the revulsion it felt to the illegal and oppressive political order created by the unilateral declaration of independence in 1965.[4]

The year 1965 was, therefore, in the eyes of the nationalists, a turning point in the life of the Church in Zimbabwe as she became outspoken against injustices and the oppression of the black majority. This was a very welcome change and augured well for the relationship between Church and state in the new Zimbabwe. The contributions of the international ecumenical bodies, such as the Lutheran World Federation and the World Council of Churches and their member Churches, to the struggle for liberation helped to create a positive attitude towards the Church and religion as a whole. No doubt reactionary elements still persisted, but the balance had tipped in support of the struggle for socio-economic and political justice. Christianity today has a place in Zimbabwe which no politician can ignore.

In addition to the two religious traditions discussed above, there is also a small Muslim community. This does not seem as yet to pose a serious challenge to Christianity. There is also a small Hindu community which is composed of people of Asian origin.

It is clear that the people of Zimbabwe are a religious people. This is not to say that there are no atheists. The majority of the people have religious connections which influence the lives of all communities. The question, then, is what is the government policy on religion? What is the relationship between religion and politics? Is there any room for religion within a Marxist-Leninist social system like the one evolving in Zimbabwe? What is the contribution of African religions and Christianity towards the formation of political thought in Zimbabwe? What is the attitude of these religious traditions towards socialism? And the creation of a one-party state? Do the current political structures allow the Church to carry out all aspects of its ministry to the people of Zimbabwe, including the prophetic ministry when it is called upon to do so? Answers to these questions should go a long way in clarifying the nature of the relationship between religion and politics as seen by Zimbabwean politicians and by the religious communities in Zimbabwe, especially the Christian community.

GOVERNMENT POLICY ON RELIGION

In order to assess contemporary religious developments in independent Africa we also have to consider the framework of government religious policies in different states.[5] In Africa state policies on religion can follow a number of different models. It is useful to make a distinction between confessional states, generally religious states, and secular states.[6] Within these models there are varying degrees of commitment. Confessional states in Africa are exemplified by Libya which has a very conservative approach. Religious states would include in their constitutions faith in God but without committing themselves to a particular religious confession. The secular states are characterized by lack of any reference to God in their constitutions. This position was clearly summarized by President Nyerere when he said:

> Tanzania has no religion; the Party has no religion; the government has no religion. But most Tanzanians are religious people and the Party and Government guarantee to each citizen the right to choose his or her own religion.[7]

The Tanzanian model is a liberal version of the secular state. Mozambique initially followed a strict Marxist approach, but appears to have relaxed this and is now currently adopting more liberal policies toward religion.

Zimbabwe is a secular state. Its position has been clarified on a number of occasions by several Government ministers, including the Prime Minister. Officially opening a Church school by the name of Mutendi School in Masvingo on April 3, 1984, the Minister of Education and Culture, Cde Dzingai Mutumbuka, said:

> Our Government believes strongly in matters of religion because of our history, and the nature of our peoples. We believe also that the spiritual dimensions of education and the development of moral character should not be neglected in our schools. Although we are against indoctrination and evangelism in our curriculum, we do want our children to explore religious beliefs and ideas, so that they arrive at a well thought-out belief system of their own and so that they learn to be tolerant and to respect those whose beliefs might differ from theirs.
>
> We therefore see religious and moral education as an essential part of our curriculum. This after all is the essence of the policy of reconciliation.[8]

The right to believe in a religion and the freedom of worship are guaranteed in the constitution of Zimbabwe. In the 1980 ZANU (PF) Election Manifesto the right to a religion and the freedom of worship are listed among what ZANU viewed as the thirteen fundamental rights and freedoms:

> The right of a person to believe in a religion is a fundamental freedom. Accordingly, a ZANU government will respect and promote the role of the Church and avoid completely interferring with the spiritual work of the Church. The Church and State must therefore feature as partners in the promotion of the welfare of the human being.[9]

Since the attainment of independence serious attempts have been made to respect this fundamental right and freedom. We are not aware of anybody which has been deprived of that right, or any religious community that has been hindered from communicating its religious beliefs or assembling its people for worship.

Government policy towards religion has tended to encourage and to support religion. The statement quoted above from the Minister of Education is clear support for this. Since Independence, religious education has been made compulsory in primary and secondary schools. Although the current syllabii are essentially Christian in content, efforts are under way to develop a multi-faith religious education syllabus. For years Christianity has monopolized the classrooms of Zimbabwe. This monopoly is now being challenged as the government has come to recognize the plural character of Zimbabwean society. Churches, through the Advisory Board for Christian Education, have objected to the multi-faith approach and insist that the Christian faith should be the basis for all religious education in Zimbabwean schools. Government policy requires that all children attend the same religious education classes, and that they be taught by qualified religious educators. Teachers should not aim to convert the children to a particular religious faith but, instead, handle the subject in such a way that the child can adopt a religious faith of his or her own choice. Reasons for such an approach are clearly stated in the quotation from Mutumbuka referred to above.

It is also interesting to observe that although the state has no official religion, religion is in the forefront of a number of state functions. State funerals for example are normally conducted in accordance with Christian burial rites. It must also be pointed out that religion is given ample time on the state run radio and television, both of which either open and/or close with prayer.

Thus it can be concluded that religion is encouraged in Zimbabwe, and, although we are dealing with a secular state, many of the politicians are themselves very religious. Most of the statements on religion from politicians have been directed to the Christian Church because it is the most powerful religious institution. The disturbing thing is that we hear more and more about politicians telling the Church what the government expects of her, what kind of a Church it desires to see in an independent Zimbabwe. In this respect the situation in Zimbabwe is not different from some other African countries. As Bishop J.H. Okullu observed, "In Africa today the state seems to be writing the agenda for both itself and for the Church".[10] While politicians tell the Church what they ought to do, as observed by one columnist in Kenya, Church leaders do not seem to have "the audacity to advise the politicians how to carry on their work".[10] What politicians in Zimbabwe are actually asking for are leaders who have a vision: they are frustrated by an African ecclesiastical leadership that is unimaginative. They are asking the Churches to be indigenous, to structure themselves in a way that would enable them to respond effectively and holistically in its ministry to the people of Zimbabwe. The Zimbabwean political leaders, although they have opted for a Marxist-Leninist inspired social system, do not view religion as "opium for the masses" or as "the sigh of the oppressed". They recognize that there are values and virtues in religion that must continue to be cultivated. It is also in this connection that attempts are being made to recover what has been lost during the period of oppression. On the whole we must say government policy towards religion is positive. Nobody is being persecuted for his or her religious convictions as has happened in other African states.[12]

CONTRIBUTION OF AFRICAN CULTURE TO AFRICAN POLITICAL THOUGHT

There can be not doubt that Western culture has had a tremendous impact on African societies and religions. Nevertheless as observed above, the traditional religions and culture are by no means a thing of the past. Most of the African political leaders grew up in environments that are traditionally African in outlook, and some of the tendencies that appear to be universal among African politicians can only be understood from the perspective of African culture and traditional religions. This includes the tendency towards one-party states, the personalization of leadership, and the desire to control all aspects of life within the state, including religious life and authority. A study of religious policies thus has to give due regard to the religious context within which it is applied.

Our political leadership in Zimbabwe is, in general, highly educated. Yet they seem to be moving in the direction of other African states. Like the rest of Africa, they are searching for a distinct African form of democracy. Disappointments with Western types of democracy has led to the conclusion that the Westminster model is no guarantee for genuine democracy. They have seen it abused, and as an alternative they turn to an African model which is based on the collectivistic or communal approach. Marxism becomes a tool with which to transform that model into a viable social system for twentieth century Africa.

As we have observed above, African people in general have great respect for elders and for those in authority. Chieftainship was inherited, and once the individual was installed as chief, he or she remained in that position for life. Installation as chief depended on the sanction of the "living dead", especially those concerned with tribal matters. Where there was a dispute as to who should become chief, the "living dead" had to be consulted. If these spirits were unable to solve the problem the Shona people of Zimbabwe sent a delegation to consult with the Voice at Matongeni.[13] African chiefs or kings wielded both the religious and what we today call the "secular" authority. In traditional societies religion was not an affair of the individual, but was viewed as a matter for the entire community. Every member of the community was obliged to participate in the faith of the community, was bound by the tradition of the ancestors, and was required to observe the regulations which were given to the family or to the community by its ancestry. It was the task of the chiefs and the elders to ensure that the faith of the community was not violated. Misconduct on the part of an individual could result in the punishment of the entire community.

The other dimension which must never be forgotten in dealing with African thought is the fact that religion permeated all aspects of African life. This all pervasive character of African religion negates any separation between the sacred and the profane or the Church and the State. Such categories do not exist in traditional African thought. Religion and politics were never viewed as two separate entities. The chief wielded both "secular" and "religious" authority. The council of elders legislated on both "religious" and "secular" matters. The terms "religious" and "secular" just did not exist. The community of the living and the "living dead" acted together, kept each other informed, and any displeasure was communicated through intermediaries. An act of war could only be declared after the consent of both communities. Spirit mediums often provided the much needed guidance in all matters.

In view of such a background it should come as no surprise when African politicians tend to tell the Churches what they should do. The political leaders see themselves as ultimately responsible for all activities within their states, hence the unwillingness or irritation on the part of most of them to accept criticism or opposition.

The phenomenon of life presidencies seems to derive also from traditional ideas of chieftainship or kingship. The political leaders know that true democracy operates on the principle of a rotating leadership, but most of them take advantage of the traditional African respect for elders and create structures that will enable them to remain in office for life. They take advantage of the ignorance of the people to consolidate their authority. Traditionally it would be a revolt against the spirit world to remove from office someone whose installation has been sanctioned by that world. I have not heard that argument used, but this could unconsciously be in the minds of the ordinary village voters when they go to the polls to vote for the only name on the ballot-paper.

The tendency towards a one-party system must again be understood in the light of that background. Traditionally, chiefs were assisted by a council of elders (*dare* in Shona). No doubt there were disagreements within the council and differences of opinion. There was no opposition for the sake of opposition. The one-party system is an attempt to model the Westminster party system along the *dare* line. The one-party terminology actually means a non-party state since within that one-party individuals stand as individuals and will be elected into parliament on the basis of their stance on specific issues. A one-party (no-party) system is meant to be a participatory form of democracy, one that involves people at grass-roots level. In a genuinely no-party participatory democratic system there should be no central party committee to field candidates for election.

It would appear that many African political leaders manipulate these traditional conceptions of leadership to consolidate their authority under the guise of developing socio-political systems that are genuinely African. As the council of elders were not elected there is always the tendency to fill parliaments with persons appointed by the life time presidents. I believe it is this traditional cultural and religious background which is being abused. Zimbabwe is a young nation and it is difficult to tell at this stage whether, in the end, the one-party system its leaders wish to adopt will indeed lead to participatory democracy or to some form of dictatorship.

CHRISTIANITY AND SOCIALISM: THE GOVERNMENT VIEW

It has been claimed by many African states that their goal is to develop socialist egalitarian societies. Many African political leaders argue that there are many socialist systems and that each state has a right to develop its own type. Nkrumah wrote:

> I have stated on many occasions that the government's policy is aimed at evolving a socialist pattern of society, no secret has been made of this fact. I have also stated that there are different paths to socialism, that each country must find its own way, and that socialism could differ in form from one country to another. Ghana intends to develop its own specialist pattern of society adoped to its own particular needs.[14]

This line of argument is repeatedly heard in Zimbabwe as politicians try to defend the socialist orientation of their policies. Hence, the Deputy Prime

Minister Cde. Simon Muzenda said to a gathering of Church people that the government's aim is to evolve a socialism that has a Zimbabwean face, and to do this "we are going to study the experiences of other countries and organizations so that we can establish a socio-economic organization which is appropriate to our socio-economic and cultural realities".[15] This means taking our concrete situation and our cultural background seriously and evolving something that is indigenous although informed by the experiences of others. Let me quote again from Muzenda:

> Zimbabwean socialism is only "Zimbabwean" in the sense that in our approach to socio-economic phenomena, we insist that Zimbabwean life itself, the hard facts of reality, our objective circumstances, should be taken into account when applying the principles of Marxism and Leninism. While we value other countries' experiences, we are, however, opposed to the importing of a carbon copy socialist system with outworn formulas, presuppositions and dogma which are irrelevant to our geo-political and historical situation. We are not doctrinaire or dogmatic.[16]

The previous colonial regimes had branded African nationalists as communists bent on establishing dictatorships. Many Church leaders in particular were very much concerned, and as a result there was some reluctance in some conservative denominations, or by individual Church leaders, to accept the political changes or to function within the new order created by the independence of Zimbabwe. The Churches therefore became a special target group for the government in its efforts to explain its policies and the kind of social system it planned to evolve.

The government believes very strongly that the Church is one of its natural allies in its efforts to create an egalitarian socialist society:

> Whatever strategy of socialist transformation the state adopts, the need to harness allies will continue forcefully to present itself. Thus, if the morality of socialism is also the morality of Christian teaching in respect of the humanistic values it cherishes, the state and the Church must see themselves more as socialist allies than as vying opponents.[17]

Christianity and socialism have much in common. In his *Theology of Promise,* President Banana is at pains to demonstrate that the Christian should feel more at home in a socialist system than in a capitalist one. As far as the government is concerned its vision of the new society and that of the Christians are identical because that vision is in both cases a vision of man. I quote again from Banana:

> The Christian vision of society is an extension of the Christian vision of man, the core of which is the primacy of the person, that is, the value and worth which the human person derives from being created in the image of God. The primacy of the human

person derives from being created in the image of God. The primacy of the human person is to be validated in history, then the concern to incarnate the Christian vision of society should be a concern for development.[18]

Development is about human beings and as such it must be concerned with the total person, his spiritual as well as his material environment. Individualism is foreign to both the Christian faith, with its concern for the neighbour, and to the African way of thinking. Hence African politicians feel morally obligated, especially in the light of their experience with a capitalist social system, to eradicate individualism. Mugabe has said:

> The elimination of an individualistic society, with its attributes of inequity and selfishness, and its replacement by a collectivistic society, with its attributes of equality and selflessness, is undoubtedly a moral philosophy. When we talk of socialism versus capitalism we are actually talking of morality versus immorality, equity versus inequity, of humanity versus inhumanity, and, I dare say, Christianity versus unchristianity.[19]

From the government perspective it is therefore a moral calling on the part of the Church to cooperate with the state, and to be involved in nation building. They insist that their form of socialism is pragmatic because it takes into account the peoples' cultural experiences, hence in his address to the Catholic Peace and Justice Commission Mugabe said:

> If Christianity's main criticism of socialism or communism is that there is too much of materialism and very little of God, my retort is: Give it a God, the God of socialism, but please never the God of capitalism! In my view Christians should feel more at home in a socialist environment than in a capitalist one.[20]

Christian values are therefore seen as being compatible with the socialist values to which the government aspires. In the past the Church has engaged in development programmes such as the building of schools and hospitals. The government would welcome partnership. The support received from the Churches during the time of the struggle for liberation has helped to create a very friendly and favourable atmophere, and as a result relations between Church and state are currently at their best.

The corner stone of the present government policies is the policy of reconciliation. President Banana devotes a whole chapter to the policy of reconciliation in his *Theology of Promise*. He sees reconciliation, as pointed out by Mutumbuka, as the

> prerequisite for unity and salvation ... Christian reconciliation means more than a limp hand-shake that tries to eliminate past wrongs; nor is it a way of ignoring contra-

dictions, but of removing them. It requires transformation, a new creation in Christ, in order for all things to be reconciled through Him (Col. 1:20). Therefore a Christian who does not strive for unity negates his very name of follower of Christ.[21]

From this perspective the government has been positive about the work of the Church, hence the pledge in the ZANU Election Manifesto to "promote the work of the Church". The question is how has the Church responded to all this and how does it view its political role in the new Zimbabwe?

CHURCH AND POLITICS

The open invitation from the government to the Churches has been met with mixed reactions. The different theological or confessional backgrounds have to a large extent determined the attitude of a particular denomination or Church leader. This has ranged from open support for government policies, including its socialist orientation, as soon as it became clear that government policy is not to create a godless society. There are others who have been suspicious and critical. The Zimbabwe Christian Council has in general been supportive.

The challenge to participate actively in development has been received positively. Churches continue to run schools, hospitals and clinics although with considerable difficulties especially in their health-care programmes. Politically, Churches have avoided criticizing the government openly, except for the Catholic Peace and Justice Commission on the situation in Matabeleland. Other Churches feel it is not yet the time for an open confrontation with the government since they have access to government officials to voice their fears and concerns or to seek clarification. A prophetic ministry can be very costly, hence it is essential that Churches are convinced of the facts before they can indulge in such a witness.

I believe the Church in Zimbabwe like any other Church in Africa is aware of its calling to be the conscience of the nation. It has a responsibility to contribute towards the formation of a just, participatory, and sustainable society. It has a role to conscientize the people so that they are aware of their political rights, so that they can speak out when they are denied those rights.

Perhaps one of the Church's most urgent and pressing tasks is the creation of structures that are more in line with the people's desire for more participation in the running of their Churches. It is regrettable that many of our African Church leaders have established themselves more as dictators, and often run the Churches as if they are private family affairs. There is also the need for a rethinking of its theology, of becoming African Churches. This is what many African governments are asking the Churches to do, and in that way people will be able to identify fully with their Churches.

NOTES

1. In view of this similarity some writers have claimed that the name Mwari is of Missionary origin. Cf. C.F. Bourdillon, *The Shona People*, Mambo Press, Gweru. This is highly unlikely.
2. Cf. Bourdillon, ibid. and others.
3. In the "Foreword" to C.S. Banana, *Theology of Promise,* College Press, Harare, 1982.
4. R.G. Mugabe, ibid.
5. On the general scene, see further *Christianity in Independent Africa,* ed. by R. Gray et al.
6. Cf. C.F. Hallencreutz, "Utvecklingsstrategi och Religionspolitik i Sydöstasien", *Kyrka och Stat,* SMT Svensk Missionstidskrift, No. 1, 1983, pp. 4-10. See the English summary p. 75.
7. Quoted from J. Henry Okullu, "Church-State Relations: The African Situation", *Church and State, Opening a New Ecumenical Discussion,* WCC Faith and Order Paper, No. 85, p. 83.
8. Press Statement
9. *1980 ZANU(PF) Election Manifesto.*
10. Op. cit., p. 80.
11. Ibid.
12. Cf. Zambia and Malawi as presented by A. Hastings in *Christianity in Independent Africa.*
13. Cf. M.L. Daneel, *The God of the Matopo Hills,* Mambo Press, Gweru.
14. Cited from J.S. Pobee, "The Fish and the Cock in Ghana, 1949-1966: A Problem of Adjustment", *The Church in a Changing Society.* Proceedings of the CIHEC-Conference in Uppsala 1977, Almqvist & Wiksell, Uppsala, 1978, p. 390.
15. Press Statement 379/83/DB, p. 6.
16. Ibid.
17. Quoted from Banana in the Press Statement 305/94/AM/SC, p. 5.
18. Press Statement 791/83/DB.
19. Quoted by Banana in Press Statement 305/84/AM/SC, p. 4.
20. Ibid.

African Church History in a New Key

Bengt Sundkler

THE TASK

"A bitter pill which the majority of writers on Christianity and missionary activities in Africa should swallow is that they have not been writing African church history." This statement by Professors Ajayi and Ayandele must serve as a challenging departure for an introduction to a discussion of a project: *a one-volume church history of Africa.* The two West African scholars develop their point by claiming that hitherto church history has been written "as if the Christian Church were *in* Africa but not of Africa". It had stressed the missionary presence while forgetting or neglecting whatever there was of an African initiative, or the African dimension of African church history.

The task of writing a Church History of Africa is to place the Church's development in African structures and to interpret the role of the Church as it speaks the new, and indeed foreign, idiom and yet discovers in itself its identity in Christ, its *new* identity. This interpretation must be set within a continental view of the emergence and growth of the Church, on the widest scale (including the universal vision of the Church "on the other side of the Waters"). The task is an ecumenical one and this, after Vatican II, is the supreme responsibility of our generation searching - or not searching - for a new ecumenical identity.

A continental panorama is necessary. An African Church History needs to be commensurate with, and part of, the hopes and vicissitudes of the continent's historical development. And yet, it is from the local perspective of village and town that a continental profile of church history can be shaped. It is the numerous encounters by groups and communities with the Christian message that provide the afflatus for Africa's church history. A history of this kind requires an "actor-centred" approach. It was often through individual and group initiatives that the Christian faith was irradiated in their own communities. These harbingers of religious change, the liberated slaves, refugees or migrant labourers, generated the feeling of numinousness which is so indivisibly a feature of the history of Christian spirituality in Africa.

IN THE OLD KEY

Is this the time for a new interpretation of the history of the Christian Church in Africa? Such surveys as we have had are Mission histories, produced in the pre-Independence period and altogether stamped by this fact. Of necessity this implied a view centred in some metropolis in the West and in certain mission societies there. Julius Richter (1922), C.P. Groves (1948-58, 4 volumes; new ed. in 1960s), Johs Beckman (1947) and G. Goyau (1948, 2 volumes) must be seen as expressions of their own time and place. Their view of Christianization was to treat it as an exclusively Western invasion of Black Africa. The continent was mapped out according to mission societies. As we criticise them it must be remembered that these scholars, two Catholic and two Protestant, were in that period ahead of their time.

Some writers publishing today deserve the attention of a critical eye. Such scrutiny can focus on two points. Firstly, there has been a noticeable emphasis on the so-called "Independent Churches", which is all very well, except that it has led to a distorted picture of African church history. The more established Western- or mission-related churches have often been relegated out of sight by a modish scholarly hunt for something "authentically African"! Yet it is the Catholic, Anglican, Lutheran, Methodist and Presbyterian (etc.) Churches to whom the overwhelming majority of African Christians have belonged and do belong. The current depreciation of these important larger churches is as mistaken as was once the neglect of the "Independent Churches". The term "Independent" has lost its glamour by now, when *all* churches are in some sense independent. Consider those great numbers! "3 000" or "6 000" have exercised their fascination for a sufficiently long time now. For South Africa one should perhaps rather refer to *one* charismatic movement - with local and personal variations. One new dimension which I stress: the Independants are not just another world, peripheral to the real thing. They are actively shaping the milieu and expectations in city locations, influencing both Catholic and Protestant.

My second observation is also a fundamental question - what *is* church history? Is there anything specific about the history of the church? Is the church anything more than just another kind of sociological construct, informed by its particular ideology; anything more than a religious department fashioned by economic forces and social tensions and struggles? The political, social and economic "background" is duly emphasised. But, this is not everything. This book is a Church History dealing with religious movements, religious institutions and radically religious individuals. I quote from Professor Sanneh to illustrate this point: "Christianity in Africa has had more than its share of the attention of Western writers, including throngs of social scientists and their disciples, most of whom are interested in everything except the Christian religion. It is as if in our concern to describe the sunlight we concentrate on the shadows, using that derivative relationship as the justification for a reductionist approach", (*West African Christianity*, 1983:xi). All I would add is that an African Church History must be about Life - or it is nothing: the struggle for Life and the Victory of Life as the Seal of a New Identity. Well then, how to convey Life, and not to miss that One Important Thing? - that is the question.

IN A NEW KEY

The old key has been dominant for a long time. It is now necessary to stress the other side. The basis of the story of the 19th century Christianization of Africa is not the mission societies, but rather, the highly mobile African communities. It is a matter of placing the conversion and the congregation in African structures and patterns, showing the African initiative within population movements.

In this connexion African church history can be related to "Refugee Movements" such as the *Mfecane* from Zululand and the Eastern Cape rippling up through East Africa via Transvaal and Mozambique and including peoples along Lake Malawi: Tonga, Tumbuka (Henga) and Ngoni. Another important structure in Southern Africa is early migrant labour (or "proto-migrant labour", if that term is preferred) with gangs of young men in the 1840s-1860s from Pedi and further north in Transvaal, going south in search of work and money - in order to buy a rifle - and in the process finding a new religion. One can see these gangs moving south on a broad spectrum from the East and the West; Botswana and Ovambo. For Southern Africa I also mention the Khoi-Nama-Griqua Church movement.

The primary importance of the *African initiative* in the founding and building up of the Church in Africa has not been sufficiently emphasised in earlier histories. For instance, C.P. Groves called his meticulous and admirably executed four volume work *The planting of Christianity in Africa* . It is characteristic that when in Vol. III. (p.174) he tackles the Church in South Africa during the last quarter of the 19th century, he writes: "By the last decades of the century the Christian cause was so well established in the South that only the general features of the situation call for review". The idea behind this position is not at all confined to Groves or his generation. It is the suggestion that the particularly interesting and important aspects and periods in African church history are those of the explorers and pioneers, the founding fathers - there were of course no founding mothers! - and that later developments everybody can somehow guess.

But one look at the situation in the church in South Africa 1870-1900 suffices to show that it was at this very time that things began to fall apart. Diamonds and gold; the first move to the city and a host of other factors - what was the church like in that situation? And I mean not only the Nehemiah Tiles and Dalindyebos and Mzimbas, for the seeds of the Independent movement were sown in those years, but the growth and tensions and aspirations of the whole Christian movement in South Africa. The point I am thus making is to stress the need for a consideration of the second and third and fourth generations in the African Church; factors of revitalisation and decline and secularisation at work in this process. This is an obvious point but has been studied less than one would expect.

Apart from the Refugee and Migrant Labour movements there are the "Returnee" movements. The liberated slaves who landed at Freetown on the West African coast came into contact with the Christian message, and a generation later many of them decided to attempt the return home, to their "roots", somewhere along the West African coast and its hinterland. These former slaves, now Christians, spread the new religion along much of the coast and interior of western Africa. Similarly, Portuguese-speaking Africans from Brazil returned across the Atlantic to Benin, Lagos and Angola, armed with their new Christian identity. In East Africa groups of liberated slaves returned from India to found Christian settlements along the coast, before attempting to journey into the East African interior. All of these "Returnee" movements were characterized by an initial hopelessness, turned into liberation with the acquisiton of a new Christian identity. These liberated slaves perforce came into contact with a wider world, obviously much larger than their ethnic identity, and this enlargement of scale and experience led to an acceptance of various innovations, not least of which were new religious commitments.

Another example of a migration leading to Christian conversion is the Fang migration through Cameroun and Gabon, resulting in the Roman

Catholic (Pallottine) Yaounde Church, American Presbyterians in southern Cameroun and American Board-French Protestants in Gabon. I call East-Central Africa's church history "The Church at the Kings Way", with its dynamic centre and origin in Buganda, leading to Anglican and Catholic Churches in Buddu, Nyoro, Toro, Ankole, Busoga, Ruanda-Burundi, Bukoba, Ushirombo and down via Fipa to Bemba in Zambia. All these societies had a similar three-tier social structure - king, nobility and commoners (and some slaves), with combinations for church adherence of the various "classes". As for North and Northeast Africa, the distinctiveness of the Churches in Ethiopia and in Egypt in the 19th century has been studied and underlined. At the end of April, 1982, I had the privilege of attending the Seventh International Conference of Ethiopian Studies at Lund, Sweden, and this gave me valuable contacts and insights into a part of Africa where, unfortunately, my knowledge is limited.

But if there is a need for a new overall look at African church history, this of course stems not only from the new studies of the 19th and 20th centuries. I must at least hint at the new image of the Donatists (W. Frend), the surprisingly rich new material on the church in Nubia and the great Belgian contributions to the study of the 16th, 17th and 18th centuries in the Congo area (Jadin, Bontnick, etc.). And in the Catholic Church of the 19th century the two great opponents or competitors, Lavigerie and Duparquet, were both stressing that their new strategies should be regarded as a "reprise", a recapture of Catholic positions lost in the Congo and elsewhere in the 18th century.

A synchronic comparison between the regions forces itself on the writer dealing with the 19th century. Now, the use of the concept of four or five regions might be disputed, for the primary unit is of course the local congregation and the local diocese or church. But, particularly for the 19th century, there is need for this concept of regions. It is suggested that the evangelistic dynamic in the various parts of Africa was sparked by an African equivalent of F. Jackson Turner's "frontier" idea. The "line of advance" streched from Sierra Leone to Nigeria, Fernando Po and Cameroun in the West, and from Cape to Zambezi and beyond in the South - sometimes referred to as the "Church's hinterland". This "frontier" - the ever receding "regions beyond" - is recognised both by the Independent Churches and the mission-related churches. At the same time we should stress the wide chronological discrepancy between the regions. West and South have a lead of at least half a century, sometimes of three Christian generations, over the Congo and the East. Then there is a similar chronological discrepancy *within* the regions. The obvious example is the difference in West Africa between the Coast with its early international and Christian contacts and Christian activity far inland.

It should be realised that there is a great difference between the local church situation and the continent-wide overview. I am always mindful of G.K. Chesterton's words: "Anything to be real must be local", and hitherto have largely kept close to this in what I have written. It is, however, one thing to establish on the local level a relationship between African society and its particular beliefs on one side and the evangelising church on the other. This has been achieved on the foundation of valuable field research, and is being done, to very great advantage. But the wider the area of reference, the more difficult it becomes. Here one is dependent on the existence of previous local and national studies. Where these are lacking later research may perhaps show that some broad conclusions will have to be modified.

On this general level I would like to be on record as stating that the immense advances represented by these studies into the history of local African cults shows that we are now on the threshold of a realistic understanding of African society and religion, and that this new advance is of importance both for a more realistic African history of religion and for the history of the church in Africa. A new image of the history of African religions emerges. Instead of the earlier image of a static, immobile religion, to be changed only through the brutal invasion of Western imperialism with its arms, and its Western faith, we are presented with an altogether dynamic, multi-faceted image of local territorial cults undergoing changes, sometimes during a matter of some four hundred years. These cults were exposed to new agencies of change in the 19th century wars, epidemics, new ecological and economic factors.

For the first and second generations the problem of *conversion* looms large. I hint at problems such as the attitude of central authority - kings, etc. - and of the especially important marginal groups. A great and difficult question is that of different degrees of receptivity in different peoples. Why were certain peoples particularly "open", "prepared" but not their neighbours? Is there any overall formula here?

The "*growth*" of the Church - a perusal of such books as have the term "growth" in their title shows that the concept itself is often forgotten. I do not of course in the first place think of numerical growth - I am sure it is hardly necessary to say that I am not a follower of McGavran or Barrett - but an interpretation which somehow conveys an understanding of the factors of growth of the local and regional church. Such factors might be: the inner cohesion and "life" of the Christian group as expressed in private or house prayers and public worship; some attempt at interpreting what is the character and charisma of the Christian experience; the interpretation of the Biblical message in and by individuals and in the corporate life of the congregation; the collective activity of the local church, relating to social commitment and other tasks; relationships to traditional and modern society.

We have stressed the role of the *African initiative* to be interpreted as far as our evidence - written and oral - allows. At the same time it must not be forgotten that the Church is a universal body. Interpreting the Church as something growing in its peculiarly West- or East- or South-African situation, this must also be related to the general international climate and to the changes of the situation. There could be a tendency in the church history writer - I experience it as a temptation - to play down the role of the westerner, to declare him or her non-existent. But we cannot so easily get around the intractable fact of the universality of the Church. And yet, I have an apophthegm on the "first missionary" in the Christianisation of Africa: That first missionary who arrived in a certain place in Africa, there to proclaim for the very first time the blessed name of Jesus - was never first! In that place there were already young men, who having been abroad had returned to their home villages, armed, perhaps, with a rifle and more importantly, with some experience of the Christian faith.

It is realised that the role of the *individual* must be seen as part of vast and fundamental movements and tendencies. Nevertheless, the question could at least be put as to whether it is not a special obligation for church history to discuss the role of the individual and the extent to which overarching trends are modified by the peculiarities of the individual. One could perhaps claim that no other movement in Africa allows the individual African personality to stand out as clearly as does the movement of the Church. And yet also here it must be regretted that the available library and archival material is limited and patchy. An example: the remarkable Catholic mass movement in Yaounde in the 1920s - 1930s was prepared by the work of a great army of Pallottine-trained (from before 1914) catechists, yet only one of these seems to be remembered by name. It is all the more interesting to learn of the Moravian biographical practice wherever they were engaged. In any case the space available for our project makes the problem of presentation and interpretation of the role of individuals an especially frustrating exercise.

Professor Ajayi has emphasised the role of the *elite*. It is a central concept of 19th and 20th century Church History in Africa, closely related to the development of mission-promoted higher education. I am not aware of a significant number of studies of the relationship of elite and mass in the mission-related church, but guess that some really important problems lie here.

The period 1920 - 1960 in African church history has a character of its own which, however, can too easily be overlooked or neglected. Squeezed in between the Pioneering Age of the 19th century (sometimes referred to as "the Great Century") and the Age of Independent Africa, the transition years would seem to lack something of the high drama of the preceding or the following periods. Yet, in the shadow of the two World Wars, this was the period when the transfer from Western mission to African Church was worked out, in endless debates at regional and local levels, in synod meetings and village councils. It was a time of widening of scale beyond the village boundaries. It was the period when the scaffolding of a church structure was erected. As a matter of course Western missionaries were in charge, although increasingly aware of the need for a determined shift of power and influence. Throughout the continent it was the period when African leaders, with growing strength and determination were looking for the "D-Day" of a transfer and towards an understanding of this new relationship. In the Catholic Church the 1950s take on such importance, with a sudden increase of Africans as bishops that Fr. Josef Metzler, O.M.I., of the Vatican Archives, refers to the period as "Africa's decade". Many Churches experienced a time of mass movement, a popular pilgrimage to the catechumenate class and the baptismal font or to the local "Jordan". It was also the period when the women were to find and indeed to assert their corporate role in the Church structures. In the 19th century the Churches in West Africa when compared with the other regions represented a distinct development of anything up to half a century ahead of the others. In the 20th century these differences were being evened out, particularly under the impact of higher education. Rapid industrialisation and urbanisation all over the continent injected a new tempo in the body politic. How far the Churches were prepared to move along to the new centres of development, together with their transient members, increasingly became a fateful question.

In the 20th century we meet with such factors as mass movements, sometimes accompanied by "revivals". One striking phenomenon is "the dormant Church" as exemplified by the mission to the Tiv: a Church which for fifty years seemed inactive and unpromising, followed by a sudden revitalisation in the 1930s - 1940s. (The role of vernacular hymns is one of the factors, or symptoms at play, but there must have been some Tiv national awakening). Are there parallels in other parts of the continent? The great problem of secularisation comes in here: the third or fourth generation Church as a lever for such development.

WRITING A CHURCH HISTORY OF A CONTINENT

I have the ambition to attempt within the limited space of some eight hundred pages, an *ecumenical* Church History of Africa. This term can mean many things to different people. I take it to mean a handbook where both Catholic and non-Catholic might find an interpretation of the essential intentions and achievements of their respective churches.

An attempt of this nature could only be made now, *after* Vatican II, the great new fact of 20th century Church History. Very generous, active and well-informed help has been given in Catholic archives and libraries in Rome, Paris and Louvain and by Catholic scholars in Africa and in various countries in the West. The attempt can never be managed to full satisfaction, but should nonetheless be made. Can it be shown, for instance, that in certain important cases a French Catholic bishop and a German Lutheran missionary laboured at about the same time in the very same area, met with much the same problems, nourished the same ambitions to study the traditional religion of the people, developed a mission policy the structures of which were very similar, yet - as far as is known - never met here on earth? There may even have been a number of such cases. In the presentation of the Catholic case, I have a tendency to present the more unfamiliar (to me) Catholic case in greater detail, with an attempt to convey the background and "local colour" while the somewhat familiar Protestant situation tends to be taken for granted. At least this has been my dilemma.

I have been surprised by the discovery of certain "mission-minded" corners of various European countries. *Not* "France" as such, but three corners therein; Brittany, Alsace and Lyon. *Not* "Germany", but that incredible Protestant Württemberg, providing missionaries to the Societies in southern and northern Germany, to Basel and to the LMS and CMS in England, at the beginning of the 19th century. *Not* "Norway", but its southwestern region, near Stavanger. The French dominance in 19th century Roman Catholic missions has also been a discovery, and likewise the role of German missionaries in the period 1894 to 1914 as well as the relative excellence of German books and mission reports by mission executives at that time. In the 1950s I collected a large quantity of material from all over Africa (in preparation for a book called "The Christian Ministry in Africa"), including such things as "The Pastor's Week", "The Pastor's Diary", and "The Pastor in Our Local Congregation" (hundreds of essays by secondary school pupils on this subject). All this material will be part of my collection of correspondence at the University Library, Uppsala and of course available to any interested reader.

The re-interpretation of the Bible message in the daily or weekly worship in the village chapel, Catholic or Protestant, belongs to this history. The role of the Bible in this history is seen as just as important for the Christian Church as the Qu'ran is for Islam. I mention the Biblical themes and archetypes (from Adam, Abraham and Moses, and the Guardians of Zion, to Bethesda and Sycar, and the Road to Damascus) re-interpreted and re-captured by preachers whose grandfathers knew the Exodus theme in their own tribal migratory traditions; the preacher and the interpreter seen against the background of speaking and Story-Telling in traditional African society, the confession for RCs and the eruptive breakthrough of confessions in Protestant revivals.

The concept of a *one-volume* piece of work is informed by educational need. Wise friends and even wiser critics have retorted, "But you need more than that! For the 2000 years of African church history you need at least three volumes!" The answer to that kind of thing is of course that you could do with thirtythree volumes and yet not have said half of what should be stated. No, all history is selection, and in this case I am convinced that definite educational needs should determine this selection. In the process of Christianisation in the 19th century we can discern a certain selectivity relating to both communicating parties, Selective Giving and Selective Appropriation.

THE HEART OF THE MATTER

Is this the time for attempting a general synthesizing of African Church History? There are possibly a number of objections to it. There is of course the most weighty one: perhaps such a church history should not be attempted by a westerner - the foreigner, the outsider, the complacent European scholar in his shielded study. I see this point almost as clearly as others do. The more I struggle with this enormous enterprise, the more I begin to understand that this task is only for someone who has real empathy with the drama of suffering and jubilation which form the African response to the Gospel of Jesus Christ. Over and against this, which is indispensable, I can only claim to have at present one advantage over my brilliant contemporaries from Africa and from the West, something which they sorely need and which is also indispensable when attempting this kind of thing: leisure. I have had the leisure of twelve years to devote to this one thing.

Of course, the Church is set in the world - even the so-called Christian village of the 19th century and the fenced-in mission station behind its hedges and walls were related to the world. The Church was placed in a social and political situation which necessarily influenced it, and conversely, the Christian group influenced the environment. But above and beyond this the Church has certain characteristics in its message, programme and growth. What is then the value of a one-volume Church History of Africa? It helps to bring out and to emphasise two overall aspects; those of continuity and change in the Church, and offers a comparison of different regions. Such comparisons help emphasise similarities and differences and thus sharpen the characterisation of each, thereby presenting a better perspective for the role of the local church.

What is the pattern in all of this? I am *not* setting out to prove any particular theory or to support any specific model. I see forces operating in different ways at different times and the divergencies may be as great as the similarities. What then is the direction of the Church's development? I see two trends: a) the role of the Church, first, as a refuge (19th century), and, then as a home (20th century - when it was not, in Dr. Busia's term, "an alien institution"), b) the Church as a lever for secularisation. Another main generalisation is that the 19th century Christianization was a youth movement (an effect of generational conflicts in African society), whereas the 20th century Christianization is primarily a woman's movement.

The Church's message and presence was seen, in the 19th century and until the First World War, as an innovation, as a chance for an alternative way of life. But the drama is that the innovation could harden into an institution. This innovation, in and through the Church of Christ, also has theological overtones. The message presented was, in the last resort, one of hope and of a new future. We are now told by an African writer that African languages did not display the dimension of the future. However that may be, the universal language of the Christian message is that of hope.

Religious Change as Transaction: The Norwegian Mission to Zululand, South Africa 1850-1906

Jarle Simensen

METHODOLOGICAL APPROACH

Missionary history has to a large extent been written by people with a missionary background and/or within the framework of academic church history. In such cases the approach has tended to be *diffusionist* with the emphasis on theological content, the build up of missionary organization and activity, and the spread of the gospel through evangelization.[1]

When Africanist historians during the last generation started to exploit the missionary material, the approach was generally more *sociological*, concentrating on the secular effects of missions, both in the social, economic and political field.[2] The research project on which the present paper is based, falls into this category.[3]

None of these approaches have produced many studies on the topic of *religious change* proper. African religious history is only in its beginning. In the South African context it can safely be stated that the topic has not been treated in a satisfactory manner in any part of the literature, at least not in the period with which this paper is concerned. The question of how local religious concepts are transformed, supplemented or discarded as a result of the encounter with an alien religion is obviously a complicated one.[4] It is generally recognized that the term "conversion", indicating a momentary and total change, may be entirely misleading. The missionaries themselves were aware of this, but their reports seldom contain any analysis of religious-psychological matters. The Norwegian reports from South Africa are conspicuously deficient in this respect. However, the fact that Africans came to the missionary stations and that a proportion of them joined the Christian congregations does provide an indicator that religious change happened, however vague the sources may be on its inner content. A first step towards an understanding of the process of religious change is to grasp hold of this indicator and focus attention on why - in the light of the prevailing social and political situation - some people changed religious affiliation while most did not.

In answering this question it will be taken for granted that Christianity may have an autonomous spiritual appeal in answering certain religious and intellectual needs better than local African religion, for instance because of its universalism, its message about life after death and the power of prayer in the struggle against evil.[5] But there is reason to doubt whether this may have been a sufficient reason for conversion in many cases. It is also difficult to imagine a *general* need for religious change in a society which is otherwise relatively stable and self-sufficient. Horton's theory about a certain correspondence between changes in the social and religious horizons of a people does, however, seem to find illustration if not confirmation in the Norwegian accounts of syncretic tendencies in Zululand towards the end of the century.[6]

The main purpose of this paper, however, is to consider religious change as part of the totality of transactions between the missionaries and the local population. Roughly speaking social-anthropological transaction theory applies the concept of the *market* to the whole area of social change, focusing on the exchange of values - material and non-material - in personal relations of reciprocity.[7] A central task is to map out the needs of the parties concerned and the means they used in the bargain for maximal need satisfaction.

The concept of "transaction" will be used to structure this paper in the belief that it may provide a clearer understanding of religious change as part of a process of social transformation. It must be stressed, however, that we are mainly borrowing some ideas and not trying a systematic application of the theory.

The basic need and aim of the missionaries in the African context was the obvious one of gaining religious adherents. Apart from the gospel they utilized a wide range of material means, goods and services, which might help to promote this aim. Some of this formed an integral part of the evangelization process, covered by such concepts as "charity" and "health". But we must ask the question whether material advantages might also be consciously distributed or withheld as part of a total transaction strategy.

On the African side the question must be asked what role material needs played in the transaction with the missionaries, in addition to the purely religious motivations touched on above. This makes it necessary to consider the total social-political situation with particular attention to basic changes which might influence individual needs. What the African partners in this transaction process had to offer was mainly religious adherence. Granted the role of autonomous religious motivation we must in addition ask whether such adherence might also be considered by the Africans as part of an exchange process and consciously given or withheld as part of a total transaction strategy.

Motives are mixed and difficult to analyse. In what follows we will mainly restrict ourselves to explicit statements in the missionary material. With regard to African attitudes and motives it is of course highly unsatisfactory to have to rely on indirect observation through the statements of missionaries whose understanding was necessarily incomplete.

TRANSACTIONS WITH THE ZULU ELITE

Let us first consider the relationship between the Norwegian missionaries and the Zulu authorities.[8] Zululand by the middle of the 19th century was an independent kingdom, but hard pressed by the neighbouring Natal Colony to the south and the Boer settlements and later republics to the north. The first approach by the pioneering missionary, H.P.S. Schreuder towards King Mpande in 1845 met with a negative response. The king was clearly afraid of a repetition of the experience of 1840-41, when an American mission under A. Grout's leadership in the south of the kingdom had become a basis for political opposition and a stepping stone for refugees from Zululand to Natal. The immediate cause for the king's change of mind and granting of permission to establish a station in Zululand in 1850 was Schreuder's ability to heal his rheumatism, and the king wished to make use of the missionary's medical expertise. But in the background political motives can also be discerned: a Norwegian mission might open up useful communication with Natal, on whose goodwill Mpande was dependent for support against the Boers. During the initial negotiations in 1845 Schreuder had not shirked from evoking the Natal threat: "... any people who time after time turned away from the gospel would certainly not remain long in the country - no! they would be torn away from their country like a useless thing and their country would be given to another people ...".[9]

Schreuder did indeed become the king's must trusted mediator with the outside world and on several occasions demonstrated a genuine identification with the Zulu kingdom and a willingness to help preserve its independence. In addition he continued his medical services in a successful manner. (When the Norwegians in 1877 considered leaving the country, they were asked to leave their medicine box behind!)[10]

As trained craftsmen the missionaries could also render useful services to the king and his court: building houses, repairing ox wagons, providing transport to and from Natal. Gifts were amply used by the missionaries to ingratiate themselves with the royal family: blankets, clothes, iron equipment, wagons, sheets and matches. The goods of civilization were presented as the fruits of Christianity: "Where have the white people got all this from, and why are they now superior to the black in so many things? Is it not the word of God which they have received which has worked these wonders among them ...?"[11] At the same time the tactical purpose of the material offer was clear: reciprocity was expected. When the king in 1867, after having declined an important request from Schreuder, went on to ask for another gift (an iron mill to grind food for the dogs he had previously received) Schreuder gave a sharp answer: "The Prince thanks me for the dogs, but what can I thank the Prince for? ... The iron mill ... will be provided in due course, when our relationship ... has become more satisfactory because it is an empty game that we should bribe (*kobana*) each other ... as long as our relationship is not in accordance with such exchange of gifts".[12]

The king's return favours were: sites for the mission stations (nine stations by 1870), permission to preach freely and occasional support in convening meetings at the king's *kraal* on a Sunday. By 1865 the influence of the missionaries at the court could also be seen in the growing habit of letting the people observe Sunday or at least work less on that day. Members of the king's household flirted with Christianity, but none converted. The king's policy with regard to conversion was clear: it was irreconcilable with citized status in the Zulu kingdom. The converts automatically lost their land and family rights, and their political privileges. This of course implied a strong political limitation on the free transaction between the missionaries and the Zulus, and acted as a powerful deterrent on religious change. By 1880 the Norwegian congregations still numbered only about 300 members.[13]

To break out of this quarantine Schreuder, in the late 1860s, proposed that the Christians, (*kholwa*), should be allowed to do regimental service, (*konza*), thus being recognized as rightful citizens. At the same time he seems to have been willing to give up the judicial "extra-territoriality" of the missionary stations. But Schreuder had no concessions to offer with regard to the religious purity of the Christians: they could not take part in regimental executions, they needed special privileges with regard to clothing (trousers) and Sunday leave, and they could not join in ceremonies and councils where traditional religion permeated proceedings. The king clearly feared that the proposed arrangement under such conditions would serve as a Trojan horse (which in a sense was also the intention) and Schreuder's proposal fell flat after a few half-hearted compromise attempts.[14]

This brought the Norwegian missionaries to a drastic change of strategy. They concluded that Zulu independence was the main obstacle to Christianization of the country and that some form of British overrule was a precondition for "freedom of religion" unhampered by political restraint.

Cetchewayo's more militant policy, *inter alia* in strengthening the regimental system during the 1870s, strained relations further and created suspicions as to the political loyalty of the missionaries. Their value as mediators and providers of modern goods was also now reduced by the fact that the British merchant-adventurer John Dunn had become the king's closest European partner. To the king the missionaries had by 1873 become "the most useless thing in the world".[15]

The basis for transactions with the Zulu authorities had thus broken down. Schreuder from now on worked actively to help establish British supremacy, and a majority group among the Norwegian missionaries took a direct part in the diplomatic preparations for the British conquest in 1879. By now the idea had also gained ground that a political "humiliation" would help create the psychological needs which might open the way for the gospel. The "national pride" of the Zulus was characterized as a "depravity" and a main hindrance to Christianization: "To human eyes it looks as if this people only through material and political humiliation can be brought to their knees and taught to seek something higher".[16]

The British conquest of 1879-80 did provide a new start for the Norwegian mission, although not one as radical as had been hoped for. The local chiefs continued in power, and no member of the Zulu elite, by 1906, had yet been won for Christianity. The cultural conservatism of the people and family pressure, continued to deter conversion almost as effectively as the king's power had done. Some of the missionaries had in fact always suspected that the resistance among the common people was as solid as that of the royal family, and that the ordinary Zulus had used the negative attitude of the "big people" largely as an excuse to avoid revealing their own lack of enthusiasm.

TRANSACTIONS WITH THE COMMON PEOPLE: THE STATION STRATEGY

By instruction from the Home Board, missionary strategy vis-à-vis the common people was to be based primarily on itinerant preaching: the "word" alone, when properly preached, would suffice to promote the cause. Practical works should be kept at a minimum.[17] This was a diffusionist approach with little understanding of local transaction relationships. Schreuder did spend much time on travel during the 1850s, and used gifts and his medical expertise to establish contacts with local communities in the same way as he had with the king. The religious offer of Christianity, however, met with little response, particularly with regard to the central concepts of sin and salvation: "Sin, what is that? Are they not devout and decent people, who don't do much evil? Why should they need Jesus to atone for their sins".[18] It was thus necessary to *inculcate* a sense of sin and thereby create the needs for the religious offer. This presupposed long and continuous contact, of a kind which could only be maintained at the mission stations.

After a while the missionaries on the spot therefore changed to a "station strategy" - like all societies in the South African field - against continuous grumblings from the Home Board. At the stations the material offer could be displayed in full. Humanitarian work was developed, particularly during the period of crisis after 1880, when new illnesses (tuberculosis, syphilis) were added to the old afflictions, and when hunger struck because of cattle confiscation during the 1880s and cattle plague, or rinderpest, in the late 1890s. The spontaneous will to help is amply documented, but the missionaries were also aware of the tactical value of such activity. Queues of patients who lined up in the mornings might have to listen to scripture reading before they were given treatment. Tooth extraction might provide an occasion to "get close to people you would not otherwise meet and ... give them God's word and ask them to come to church etc".[19]

The most important means for drawing people to the station was paid work. There was a tendency to keep a maximum number of servants (a record of 60-70 at one station) in order to provide recruits for the congregation. Declarations about religious motives from the recruits in such cases had to be taken with reservation. An English missionary reported from a visit to a local chief: "In the morning his son came out and said: We are believers. When asked what this meant, the answer was: I would like to work with you. And this is a type of joyful belief among many of those who approach the recently arrived missionary".[20] The market for local agricultural products provided by the station was also highly valued.

Attention at service was the main reciprocation of those Zulus who were drawn into interaction with the missionaries in this manner. How strong the idea was of a concrete transaction is amply documented. To attend Sunday service was termed "to do Sunday work" (*sonda*). At Empageni in 1856 a missionary had refused to buy agricultural products which he did not need from some Zulu women. Their reaction was as follows: "Look, we are your people, haven't you seen us at service? Look how long we have *sonda*, so many (three fingers in the air) are the Sundays that we have *sonda* with our families, we now thought you would buy from us amply, but look, you refuse and turn away, what wrong have we done? How have we sinned? How can we now come and listen to God's Word? It seems you do not want us to *sonda*!"[21] Oftebro thought this was typical of people's attitude. At the same time Larsen at Umpumulo reflected that *nobody* came to service just to listen to God's Word. Every autumn attendance increased, because the people wrongly believed the missionaries would not buy their maize if they did not turn up on Sundays. There were indications that people came to *sonda* out of religious motives, but then of a special character: they feared there might be strong spiritual powers behind the missionaries. *Sonda* might thus be benificial to the harvest, whereas abstention might lead to "rats and birds" in the field.[22]

In the long run the main instrument for evangelization, in Zululand as in the rest of Africa, were the mission schools. [23] The missionaries were strongly aware of their strategic importance, and were at times willing to pay cash to persuade families to send children to the school. Pressure was put on the paid labourers and servants to attend school, and the logic of this transaction was understood. On one occasion neighbours of a mission station, who had refused schooling made the following comment: "It is natural that those who work for pay at the station observe Sunday and that those who want to, 'learn', for the white man who pays them for their work can also give them the work 'to learn'. But we who are not in his pay, why should we observe Sunday, and that with a white man who (in their opinion) is on the side of the Boers".[24]

After the conquest of 1880 the missionaries received a new strong card in the transaction game in that they were given rights of property over considerable land areas around the stations. This attracted people in search of land and also made it possible to apply pressure for good purpose. On several occasions parents who refused to send their children to school were threatened by eviction: "The Location had been given to the mission by the government and the government expected that people who settled there would receive education".[25]

Because of the large white population and the policy of segregation, the mission schools in South Africa probably did not have the same career or advancement value as in the rest of the continent. Still it was an indubitable advantage on the job market, particularly in the towns. This was widely realized as Zululand was increasingly drawn into the money economy towards the end of the century. In particular knowledge of English was highly valued, but here the Norwegian schools were deficient. They had started with Zulu as the means of instruction, but were obliged to change into English because of parental demands and the danger of losing pupils to mission societies with English-speaking schools. Pressure from the colonial authorities and the fear of a state school system in the case of non-cooperation also played a role. The extra effort involved was deplored by the Home Board, who maintained that "it was not necessary to know English to be saved".[26] Many Zulu parents still continued to resist sending their children to the missionary schools, not always because they lacked a sense of the value of education, but because they feared that the school would be the first step towards a religious change which would "snatch" the children away from their parents. This was of course a concrete reading of their main intention. This was an example of the paradox that evangelization might hamper - and not further - the progress of civilization! But again it must be emphasised that a transaction model does not cover everything. There is ample evidence that the missionaries genuinely believed both in the independent value of education and its secular function in strengthening the Zulus "in the competition with the white population", and in creating a sense of self-awareness so that the Africans would not allow themselves to be treated as "willing tools".[27] Christians from the mission stations became the leaders of early nationalist activity.

An important attraction of the early mission stations in Zululand as in the rest of Africa, was their "extra-territoriality" - taken in a wide sense of the word - which meant that they became a refuge for people at odds with Zulu society. Schreuder had taken in refugees from the Zulu civil wars as early as in 1856, and throughout the period up to 1880 refugees from the Kingdom continued to use the stations as stepping stones on their way to the Natal colony. A considerable number of the refugees were young women. They might be young girls in love with men at the stations (the first convert belonged to this group, and one of the missionaries in 1871 wrote that there was almost always a love story behind the conversion of a young girl to Christianity.[28] Escape from forced marriages was another motivation. But the charity, relative comfort, freedom from field work and respectful treatment must have appealed to women of all age groups, not least the elderly who were often neglected, maltreated or accused of witchcraft. After the arrival of one such witchcraft suspect Astrup commented he could find "no inner conviction or desire for the word of God" in her, but he gave her asylum because she said "she would convert to God".[29] In such cases the religious motive clearly could not be as important compared with that of material attraction. On the other hand such refugees were dependent on the missionaries to a particular degree and presumably, therefore, specially amenable to their teaching.

From the perspective of Zulu leaders the refugees confirmed their suspicion that the mission stations undermined local authority by providing an outlet for oppositional and criminal persons. A delegation from the king in 1877 complained to the Natal Secretary for native affairs, Sir Theophilius Shepstone: "If a Zulu does something wrong, he immediately goes to the mission station saying he wants to become a Christian, if he wants to elope with a girl, he becomes a Christian, if he wants to avoid military service, ... he dons clothes and becomes a Christian, if he is an 'umtagati' (one who does evil and hurts others), he becomes a Christian".[30]

THE CHRISTIAN CONGREGATIONS

A decisive stage in the transaction process was reached when Zulus after long-term contact with the missionaries went over to the Christian religion (*wela*, i.e. set across) through babtism. The depth of the religious change was an open question. The candidate must persuade the missionary that his intention was sincere, and then go through a special preparation course for baptism. Literacy was not demanded, but the candidates must be well acquainted with the five parts of Luther's small catechism, and know questions and answers from Pontoppidan's commentary by heart. At times the missionaries were in doubt about the sincerity of the conversion, and many backsliders showed that such doubts were justified. On the other hand the Norwegian mission produced its first and only martyr in 1874, when Umakumuzela, who had fled from regimental service, was caught by a group of royal executioners and killed, according to the missionary report "happy in his belief in his Saviour".[31]

It is obvious that religious motives must be given due emphasis at this stage of the transaction process. It is probably easiest to explain the religious conversion of those who came to the stations as refugees. They were so to speak products of internal tensions in Zulu society - political opposition, generational and gender conflicts - and must themselves frequently have experienced strong psychological tensions. They might have been haunted by a fear of death, a troubled conscience - in some cases possibly caused by accusations of witchcraft - and needed prayer as a protection against the forces of evil. In joining the Christian congregations they achieved not only material, but also spiritual security and probably a feeling of atonement. Baptism was in addition a symbolic confirmation of their alliance with the missionaries and other Christians in a new, chosen group. These were people who had little to lose in the old society and everything to gain from the new community. In Norman Etherington's words, freely transcribed from the Sermon on the Mount: "They were the poor in spirit - kingdomless men who were glad enough to find a place in the kingdom of Heaven. They were the meek - landless men who longed to inherit the Earth. Having been reviled, or persecuted, or having had all manner of evil said against them falsely, they must have been heartened by the thought that an act of belief would transmute them into the salt of the Earth and the light of their world".[32]

But the change of religion could also give practical advantages: Christians were given priority with regard to paid labour and land rights at the stations. Those who were interested in trade and transport achieved greater freedom of movement, as they were entitled to cross back and forth over the border to Natal. These privileges were not shared by those Zulus who came to the stations without joining the congregations. The technical skill of the Christians could be seen from the standard of their houses. In the fields the plough made a spectacular difference, and it was claimed that "the Christians could frequently hear people talk with envy about their big fields, ample food and other advantages in *konze abelunga* (serving the whites)".[33] Diligent and entrepreneurial persons were given the chance to amass private capital. Schreuder perceived the links between moral perfection and material welfare in terms reminiscent of Max Weber, while Prince Cetshwayo condemned Christian behaviour: "... they do nothing but work ... and do not serve either their chief or king. They only live for their own success".[34]

To try and define the weight of material advantages compared to those of religious motives in conversion is clearly an impossible undertaking, as is - in principle - all motive analysis. Etherington has categorized a sample of 177 cases of conversion from other mission societies in the South African field where the motives for joining the Christian congregation were described in the missionary reports. 12% of these conversions were said to be caused by religious interest alone, 26% by the desire for paid work, 33% by the need for a place of refuge at the station (of which 3% fled from accusations of witchcraft and 10% from prearranged marriages). 15% accompanied parents or relatives and 14% followed the missionary from his earlier station.[35] Such figures must be taken with due reservations, but they give at least an indication of the main categories of motives. We may assume that the material motives were most important in establishing the first contact with the missionaries and the religious motives more prominent at the time of baptism and inclusion into the congregation. Children of Christian parents were of course assimilated into a congregation through childhood and education.

A sense of disappointment and pessimism pervades the Norwegian missionary reports from Zululand right up to the end of the century. In the period up to 1880 this related partly to the quality of the converts: "Only a few from the most common classes, sick, frail and poor, joined the congregations, people whom the Zulu chiefs were only too pleased to lose. They were good-for-nothing and could go where they wanted".[36] Many of the Christians in the early congregations were also strangers from Natal or people from other stations in Zululand, which increased their estrangement from local society. The mixed background, the losening of customary ties and the lack of firm judicial arrangements at the stations frequently created an atmosphere of strife and internal disorder which drove the missionaries to despair. Some went so far as to maintain that the character of the Christians and of station society was a liability in the transaction process with the Zulus: "Instead of demonstrating a burning spirit the Christians deterred the heathen by their poor behaviour ...".[37]

After 1880 there was a steady growth in the Norwegian congregations from about 300 in 1880 to 1 100 in 1890, 2 600 in 1900 and about 5 000 in 1906. A breakdown of these figures, however, explained the reasons for continued missionary disappointment: about 50% of the growth was caused by self-recruitment through children of congregation members. In explaining this lack of appeal, the total situation within which the transaction process took place must be considered. We have seen that the British conquest was considered a precondition for further missionary progress. Similarly the view gained ground that the traditional economic system must be broken, both in order to remove some of the cultural hindrances to conversion like polygamy and the bride-price (*lobola*), and in order to promote inclusion into the South African money economy and thus create greater need for the material offer of the missions: "Thus even taxation serves to drive the people to listen to God's word".[38] Even gold mining, with its attendant effects of depletion of the rural population and exposure to the sinful aspects of modern civilization might have positive consequences: "This also serves to break down traditional rights, prejudices and customs among the Zulus. Thus the gold Mammon, which frequently brings so much evil, may indirectly serve the progress of the Gospel".[39]

Most striking in retrospect is the satisfaction with which some of the missionaries greeted the destruction of the Zulu economy and the material distress that befell the country after the British conquest and the civil wars of the 1880s. This was the humiliation thesis in a new version: "... it might again be proven that when a people has been thoroughly humiliated and their national pride broken down, then in all its abjection and submission they may be willing to listen to Him who invites all who are burdened to come to him and seek rest for their souls".[40] It was reported that this made "good sermon material".[41] Probably this attitude may be partly explained with reference to the strongly pietist aspect of the Norwegian Lutheran milieu which emphasised that distress and crisis might create an awareness of sin and thus be a way to salvation. Schreuder himself, however, who had broken with the Norwegian Missionary Society in 1873, did not articulate this "humiliation thesis" and his successor Nils Astrup positively condemned it. There were other exceptions to this attitude within the NMS missionary group.

One aspect of anthropological transaction theory concerns the adjustment of strategies on the basis of feedback from the other party. On the missionary side this only happened to a minimal degree. The Home Board continued to hold back on grants for practical works, and in 1887 went so far as to fire one missionary, Dr. Oftebro, who was overzealous in this respect. On the central question of baptism requirements the general instruction gave no room for adjustment: "No heathen customs must be tolerated".[42] Most aspects of Zulu culture came under the definition of sin, based not only on general Christian but also on specific European cultural criteria. This naturally kept the cost of religious change high in terms of conflict within family and local society: "If they were allowed to live in polygamy and retain their dear heathen customs untouched, I think many would have been willing to pay an outward allegiance to Christianity".[43] One important point where a compromise for a long time seemed necessary was the custom of bride price (*lobola*). But the Natal government had outlawed the custom, and when Zululand was incorporated into the colony in 1897 the Norwegian missionaries' annual conference followed suit in 1900. The transaction cost of the measure was illustrated when the government started registration of the Christians at Umpumulo station in 1898 with a view to putting the law into operation: station members who were not baptised immediately reacted by abstaining from school and baptism preparations. Only a few old women remained.[44]

AFRICAN CHRISTIAN ENTREPRENEURS

In anthropological theory the "entrepreneur" occupies a central role in the transaction process, promoting change and enhancing personal profit by mediating between the different needs and value systems of the parties concerned. In the Zulu missionary situation the closest approach to this function was represented by some of the Christian converts who tried to straddle the gulf between the congregation and Zulu society during the early mission period. Let us by way of illustration take a look at two brothers, Isac and Paul, who were among the first baptised.[45] They were sons of a well-known rainmaker in Zululand, who after some unsuccessful practice had fled to Natal. He had many wives and innumerable children. To them he recommended conversion, while he himself continued to make good money as a rain-maker in Natal. Isac and Paul had, according to Schreuder, inherited their father's "restless intelligence and flair for lofty projects".

Immediately after his baptism Isac started to exploit the economic opportunities open to a Christian. With money he earned at the mission station he travelled to Durban, bought goods, returned to Zululand, and bought up cattle which he then exported to Natal. His economic success seems to have increased his self-confidence to such a degree that he ignored the moral rules regulating station society. In 1865 he was excluded from the congregation at Eshowe because of drunkenness. At this time his brother Paul also joined in the transport and trade activities because he was no longer satisfied with the 10 shillings per month which he received from the missionary, Oftebro. In 1869 Oftebro reported that Paul had put much effort into helping Isac to build himself a brick house, European style, at Eshowe station.

When Christians for a while, in 1870, had the chance to do service to the king, Isac and Paul took the opportunity to cultivate a large field for Cetshwayo with their oxen and ploughs against payment in cattle. They were also sent to Natal to buy blankets for the prince. One year later their business activity was so extensive that they had to hire labour. Through these services the rainmaker's sons ingratiated themselves with Cetshwayo. In this manner they managed to obtain permission to establish a large cattle farm in the border district towards Natal, close to the Tugela river, where they also cultivated large fields. A third brother, Johannes Haugvaldstad, one of Schreuder's first converts, then joined the firm.

One tempting opportunity to convert profit into status based on the criteria of Zulu society was to take several wives. At his cattle farm Isac entered into a relationship with a girl who was to become his wife number two. To deceive Oftebro and the congregation he brought along this girl to Eshowe and registered her as a school pupil. He declared himself free from sin, and joined in Holy Supper as usual. When the truth was brought home to Oftebro through rumours and reports from other Christians, Isac defended himself by pointing to Abraham and Isac in the Old Testament who had also taken several wives.

There was a sudden halt in Isac's hectic activity when he accidentally shot himself in the leg. He was then brought to Eshowe as a cripple. Here he became a repentant sinner and after long and good treatment he was healed. But the stay at the station had not killed his spirit of independence. As soon as he was restored to health, he went away to "Sodom" - the cattle farm at Tugela - without being present when his child was baptized at Eshowe. In "Sodom" he married his second and third wives, and his brother Paul planned to follow his example.

However, the rainmaker's sons also ran into conflict with Zulu society because of their trading activities. And since they had also broken with the Christian congregations, only one possibility was left: they fled with all their belongings and all their wives, including the baptized, to Natal and settled down close to Umpumulo. The last missionary reports on the two brothers were pathetic. When Paul returned illegally to Eshowe, he was asked by Oftebro: "Where are you now?" The answer was: "I am nowhere". Oftebro reports that he looked "dark and unhealthy. He is said to suffer terribly from pangs of conscience, and tries to drive this away by *insangu*, smoking a narcotic hemp - so that he occasionally looks as if he is losing his mind".[46] Oftebro was also visited by one of Isac's wives, the first and legal one, Rebecca, who told the missionary that her husband still read the Bible and prayed to God. He still counted himself a believer and comforted himself that he would be received by God in heaven just as Abraham and other polygamists from the Bible.

To some degree all Christians must have been "entrepreneurs" as no conversion can have been absolute in the sense of a total change of personality and an abrupt end to all contact with local society. As Christian ideas spread in Zulu society outside of the congregations and Christians, partly because of their increased number, began to stay with their families after conversion without moving to the mission station, the distance between the two worlds was reduced and a far more differentiated process of interaction became possible. This clearly eased religious change, but at the same time probably also changed the *de facto* content of the Christian religion in the African context.

CONCLUSION

The special value of the Norwegian missionary material from South Africa lies in the fact that it throws light on the topic of religious change in an opening phase of the encounter between European civilization and a politically independent and relatively selfsufficient African society. Christian missions thus became part of a comprehensive process of political and economic change to which they contributed and which in its turn created new conditions for their own activity. In such a situation it becomes particularly clear how closely African religious change was tied up with the process of social transformation.

Our approach to the question of religious change has been a partial one. We have concentrated on its outward manifestations in the form of change in religious adherence, registered in the growth of mission station society and Christian congregations. Without discarding purely religious motives we have tried to define the role played by African needs - material as well as political - and the missionary offer in this respect. The concept of transaction - taken from social-anthropological theory - has been used throughout to grasp the totality of the relationship between the missionaries and their African partners.

By way of circumscription this "external" approach may also provide some indications about the *internal* aspect of African religious change. In some cases it seems clear that the material factors provide sufficient explanation for a change in religious adherence, as for instance with the refugees who declared conversion and joined the congregations. Change of beliefs could not always be abrupt and total, a fact that the missionaries were painfully aware of. And elements of traditional Zulu religion did continue to surface in the congregations, for instance in the form of witch-hunting at times of strains and conflict. On the other hand the Norwegian material provides evidence of change in traditional Zulu religion, partly under Christian influence, outside of the congregations.

The Zulu case thus provides another example of what has gradually emerged as a main research topic, namely the continuity of African religious history. To elucidate this topic will require an interdisciplinary approach and a stronger research contribution by Africans than has been the case up to now.

NOTES

NMT = *Norsk Missions-Tidende.* (The Journal of the Norwegian Missionary Society.) Most of the missionary reports from South Africa up to 1906 were published in this journal.

MB = *Missionsblad/Zuluvennen.* (The Journal of the "Norwegian Church Mission to South Africa by Schreuder", after Schreuder's break with the NMS in 1873.)

1. A classical survey is C.P. Groves, *The Planting of Christianity in Africa, I-IV,* London, 1945-58. The standard account of the Norwegian missionary endeavour in South Africa is O.G. Myklebust, *Det Norske Misjonssellskaps Historie, III, South Africa,* Stavanger, 1949, and the same author: *H.P.S. Schreuder: Kirke og misjon,* Oslo, 1980.

2. A general survey of historical research based on missionary material is R. Strayer: "Mission History in Africa: New Perspectives on an Encounter", *The African Studies Review,* Vol. 19, No. 1, 1976.

   Examples of studies of mission and social change from different parts of Africa are R. Oliver: *The Missionary Factor in East Africa,* London, 1952; J.F.A. Ajayi: *Christian Missions in Nigeria, 1841-1891,* London, 1965; R.I. Rotberg: *Christian Missionaries and the Creation of Northern Rhodesia ,* Princeton, 1965; Bonar A. Gow: *Madagascar and the Protestant Impact,* London, 1969.

   For studies of South African missions see Norman Etherington: *Preachers, Peasants and Politics in South-East Africa 1835-1880: African Christian Communities in Natal, Pondoland and Zululand,* London, 1978, and his bibliography on previous works. In addition the following articles have given perspectives: B. Hutchinson: "Some Social Consequences of 19th Century Missionary Activity among the South African Bantu", *Africa,* Vol. 27, No. 2, 1957, and C. Tsehloane Keto: "Race Relations, Land and the Changing Missionary Role in South Africa: A Case study of the Zulu Mission, 1850-1910", *The International Journal of African Historical Studies ,* Vol. 10, No. 4, 1976. A study of American Zulu Mission is L.E. Switzer: "The Problems of an African Mission in a White-Dominated, Multi-Racial Society: The American Zulu Mission in South Africa 1885-1910", Ph.D., Los Angeles, 1971.

3. "Norwegian Missions in African History. Madagascar and Zululand in the 19th century", *Zululand,* Vol. I, ed. by Jarle Simensen; *Madagascar,* Vol. II, ed. by Finn Fuglestad and Jarle Simensen, Trondheim, 1983.

   This is a team project supported by the Norwegian Research Council for the Humanities, partly based on the following cand. phil. theses (available on microfiche at the University Library, University of Trondheim):

a. Vidar Gynnild, "Norske misjonærer på 1800-tallet. Geografisk, sosial og religiøs bakgrunn", Trondheim, 1981.
b. Per Hernæs, "Norsk misjon og sosial endring. Norske misjonærer i Zululand/Natal 1887-1906", Trondheim 1978.
c. Øystein Rennemo, "Menalambaopprøret, Madagaskar 1895-97", Trondheim, 1980.
d. Edgar Scarborough, "Evangelisering, modernisering og rikssamling. Samarbeidet mellom norske misjonærer og styret i Hovariket på Madagaskar i oppbyggingen av skoleverket i provinsene Betsileo og Imerina, 1867-1890", Trondheim, 1975.
e. Endre Sønstebø, "Fortropper for europeisk imperialisme. - Norske misjonærer i Zululand 1850-1880", Trondheim, 1973.
f. Thomas M. Børhaug, "Imperialismens kollaboratører? En analyse av norske misjonærers holdning og rolle under den europeiske etableringsfasen i Zululand 1873-1890", Trondheim, 1976.
g. Kåre Lode, "Tilhøvet mellom norske misjonærer og styresmaktane på Madagaskar 1867-1895", Bergen, 1971.
Most of the material for the present article comes from the following two contributions to Zululand,Vol. I from this research project, J. Simensen with V. Gynnild, "Norwegian missionaries in the 19th century: organizational background, social profile and world view", and J. Simensen e.a., "Christian missions and socio-cultural change in Zululand 1850-1906. Norwegian strategy and African response".
In what follows references to the original material are only given for quotations.
4. For literature on African religious change see W. de Craemer, J. Vansina and R. Fox, "Religious movements in Central Africa", Comparative Studies in Society and History, Vol. 18, No. 4, 1976; W.M.I. Van Binsbergen of R. Bujtenhuis (ed.), African Perspectives, Vol. 2, 1976 (theme number about religion); T.O. Ranger, The Historical Study of African Religion , Berkeley 1972; and T.O. Ranger, Themes in the Christian History of Central Africa, London, 1975. A study of Zulu syncretism is Bengt M. Sundkler, Bantu Prophets in South Africa, London 1961, 2nd edition.
5. Richard Gray, "Christianity and Religious Change in Africa", African Affairs, Vol. 77, No. 306, January 1978.
6. R. Horton, "African conversion", Africa, Vol. 41, No. 2, 1971. NMS Visitation report, 2 September 1891, describes syncretic tendencies.
7. Fredrik Barth's transaction theory is found in his Sosialantropologiske problem, Stockholm, 1971. A discussion of the justification of a broader theoretical perspective in the study of mission may be found in T.O. Beidelman, "Social Theory and the Study of Christian Missions in Africa", Africa, Vol. 44, 1974, pp. 235-49 with comments by Norman Etherington in "Social Theory and the Study of Christian Missions in Africa: A South African Case Study", Africa, Vol. 47, No. 1, 1977, pp. 31-39.
8. The standard introduction to South African economic and social history is M. Wilson and L. Thompson, The Oxford History of South Africa, Vols. I and II, Oxford, 1969 and 1973; Jeff Guy, The Destruction of the Zulu Kingdom, London, 1979, and the background chapters in Shula Marks, Reluctant Rebellion. The 1906-1908 disturbances in Natal, London, 1970. A detailed analysis of the relationship of the Norwegian missionaries and the Zulu authorities is found in Per Hernæs, "The Zulu Kingdom, Norwegian Missionaries and British Imperialism, 1845-79", contribution to Jarle Simensen (ed.), Norwegian Mission in African History, Vol. I, Zululand , Trondheim, 1973.
9. NMT, February, 1846, reprinted in MB, 1880, pp. 122-143.

102

10. Robertson to Bulwer, 4th of July 1877, Government House Papers, Pietermaritzburg, Folio 1397, quoted in N. Etherington, *Preachers, Peasants and Politics*, op. cit., note 11, p. 79.
11. NMT, May 1868.
12. NMT, October 1867, p. 295.
13. O.G. Myklebust, op. cit., p. 89.
14. The *kholwa-konza* question is treated in detail in Per Hernæs, "The Zulu Kingdom ..., op. cit.
15. NMT, 1873, p. 118.
16. NMT, February 1860.
17. *Rules and Regulations for the NMS missionaries*, quoted in NMT, March 1852, p. 169.
18. NMT, 1901, p. 238.
19. MB, 1889, p. 119.
20. Marsh to Anderson, August 1849, ABC 15.4. IV, quoted in Etherington, op. cit., p. 148.
21. NMT, July 1856, p. 7.
22. NMT, May 1868, p. 141.
23. The fullest account of the school policy of the Norwegian mission is found in Per Hernæs' cand.philol. thesis *Norsk misjon og sosial endring. Norske misjonærer i Zululand/Natal 1887-1906*, Trondheim, 1978.
24. NMT, 1887, pp. 231-232.
25. Visitation Report, Stavem, u. d. 1890.
26. O. Gjerløw, "Beretning vedkommende Sekretærens Reise til Missisonsmarken i Zululand og Natal 1887-88", pp. 22-23.
27. MB, 1894, p. 178 and NMT, 1894, p. 405 and 1905, pp. 564-65.
28. NMT, October/November 1867 and June 1871, reports from Empageni and Entumeni.
29. MB, 1894, p. 166.
30. Quoted in C. Tshebane Keto, "Race Relations ..., op. cit, p. 608.
31. NMT, November 1874, p. 402 and NMT, August 1877, pp. 303-304.
32. N. Etherington, op. cit., p. 114.
33. NMT, August, 1877, p. 302.
34. Cetshwayo in Robertson to Colenso, 2 January 1863, SPG, D 25, quoted in Etherington, op. cit., p. 192.
35. Ibid. pp. 102-103.
36. O. Stavem, *Ett bantufolk og kristendommen*, Stavanger, 1915, p. 63.
37. MB, 1904, p. 158.
38. NMT, December 1855, p. 90.
39. MB, 1887, p. 84.
40. NMT, 1889, p. 3.
41. NMT, 1895, p. 306.
42. *Rules and Regulations*, op. cit.
43. NMS's 55th Annual Report, p. 2.
44. NMT, 1898, p. 206.
45. Isac and Paul's biography plus those of other Zulu Christian "entrepreneurs" can be found in E. Sønstebø: "Fortropper for europeisk imperialisme. Norske misjonærer i Zululand 1850-1880", Trondheim, 1973, cand. philol. thesis under the project "Norwegian Mission in African History", op. cit.
46. NMT, July 1875.

The Arab Influence on Madagascar

Ludvig Munthe

I would like to draw your attention to some unrecognized material concerning Arab influence in Madagascar. In recent years there has been an attempt to publicize the relatively hidden Arabic material in Madagascar.

Normally, when referring to Madagascar, we do not connect her culture or her language to the Arabs or any other Semitic group. The relationship between Madagascar and East Africa is better known. There are ethnic and linguistic links between Africa and the west-coast peoples of Madagascar. Some Bantu and Swahili words are still used in Madagascar, although African language influence is relatively small.

A more important influence on Madagascar came from the distant islands of Indonesia: Borneo, Java and especially Sumatra. There is no longer any doubt that the people of Madagascar and the main culture of the island originated in Indonesia. This has been proved by the existence of "Indonesian" houses, tools, and by the type of agricultural practices used in the island. The linguistic relationship has been shown by one of my colleagues in Stavanger, Dr. O. Chr. Dahl, in his studies concerning *Manjaan et Malgache*, and in his recent book on the Austronesian languages.

THE ARABIC-MALAGASY MANUSCRIPTS

It is well known that Arab merchants, through the centuries, have reached Madagascar as well as other countries in the Indian Ocean. Therefore, it is not surprising that Arab words for money, trading, writing exist in todays language in Madagascar. As an example we may mention *soratra (manortatra)* which means writing (to write). Evidently soratra has a certain connexion with sourat in the Koran.

It is also well known that small groups of Arabs reached Madagascar several hundred years ago and settled on the northern and the eastern coast of the island. The legacy of that settlement can be seen today in the faces of some of the Antaimoro people, which reveal the Arab physiognomy and profile. A few of them have also kept the religion of their forefathers, dressing like Arabs and considering themselves to be Muslims, although they know very little about Islam.

We don't know exactly when these Arab groups came to Madagascar, married Malagasy women and settled among the islanders, but probably they arrived between the tenth and the thirteenth centuries. What we do know is that the immigrants brought the first knowledge of literacy to Madagascar. They taught their children the Arabic alphabet in order to transmit Islamic scriptures and traditions, and to keep the community together. By slightly adapting their Arabic alphabet to the sounds of the Malagasy language, the Antaimoro of the east coast were the first group to prepare a written script for the Malagasy language.

The name *sorabe* which derives from *soratra*, which has already been mentioned, raises the still unanswered question of the possible existence of an earlier unknown Malagasy script of *"small"* letters. What we, however, do know is that the *sorabe* was the only alphabet known in Madagascar at the beginning of the 19th century. Only during the last decades of the eighteenth century was the king of Antananarivo in Madagascar informed of the existence of this alphabet - hundreds of years after the establishment of the small literate group on the coast.

King Radama the First (1818-1828) learned, as a boy, to read and write *sorabe* from a *katibo* Antaimoro. His interest in literacy led him to study European writings as well. In 1823 the first national monarch, King Radama I, decided to adopt the Latin alphabet, prepared and proposed by David Jones of the London Missionary Society. Jones himself studied the *sorabe* in Antananarivo. When preparing the translation of the Bible he tried to use the *sorabe* alphabet. At the same time the directors of the LMS and those of the British and Foreign Bible Society also studied the possibility of using the *sorabe* alphabet. They benefitted from the arrival of a young Antaimoro, sent to London to study industry.

A copy of one of the demonstration papers given to them by the young Verkee (Ravarika), probably before 1820, is attached to this paper.

This document contains three verses in *English* from the English Bible, written in the *sorabe* alphabet. He also rendered the same verses in French and Malagasy versions, all written in *sorabe*. As far as the Malagasy version is concerned, it represents the first serious attempt to translate parts of the Bible into Madagascar language.

The experiment in using this script was not successful and London decided to ask Jones not to use the *sorabe*. Supported by the directors of the Mission, Jones proposed the adoption of the Latin alphabet, and this was accepted by the king. Thus Jones influenced the future of Madagascar's cultural and religious evolution. Abandoned by the Antananarivo kings the *sorabe* lost its role as a major factor in determining Madagascar's evolution and future.

As the *sorabe* represents the earliest texts written in the Malagasy language, mixed with pure Arabic passages from the Koran, it is of vital importance for the history of Madagascar's past. This Arabic-Malagasy literate tradition is little known in Europe and, indeed, in Madagascar.

During the last century the Antaimoro tribe hesitated as to whether they should divulge their secret of literacy. Many of them felt it was against the wishes of their forefathers to teach others the secrets. Not only the surviving texts but even the knowledge of the sacred *sorabe* letters was kept hidden. During the colonial period (from 1895) the French succeeded in obtaining some manuscripts. With their knowledge of Arabic, and contacts with Algiers university, some French scholars presented a few manuscripts. But most of the manuscripts were hidden away and forgotten in European and Malagasy archives and museums.

Today young Malagasy students studying linguistics learn to read *sorabe*. Although the university and the nation are now administered by Malgasies themselves, they have not yet succeeded in conserving the manuscripts, which are still dispersed in Antaimoro villages, under grassroofs and in holes in the cliffs or in the woods.

About a dozen individuals in every generation are still charged by the Antaimoro people with the heavy responsibility of guarding and handing the manuscripts to the next generation. Some of these individuals are aware of the unsatisfactory way in which these manuscripts are kept. But they are committed to their responsibilities, and ancient laws and restrictions prevent them from taking the proper steps to protect the manuscripts.

Because of this Malagasy scholars are unable to benefit from these written sources for the history, religion and language of Madagascar. The prospects of saving the manuscripts are bleak. In one small village in 1973, ten manuscripts were destroyed by fire. The keepers did not even know the contents.

In 1972-73 it was estimated that about one hundred manuscripts were still in existence. There might even be more. If these manuscripts should perish

Madagascar will loose important knowledge about its religion and its history.

It is possible that some of these manuscripts can yet be saved. But at the moment we have to base our study of this ancient Malagasy source on what is already located. A survey in Malagasy and European museums and archives last year reported that more than 7 000 pages of *sorabe* documents still exist. Madagascar scholars hope for a European initiative in making this treasure available for research. This is understandable, as the majority of the manuscripts are hidden in Europe.

THE CONTENT OF THE SORABE MANUSCRIPTS

After taking into consideration the existence of some falsified texts, we find that the genuine manuscripts inform us of three items. Because the *sorabe* is written phonetically the Malagasy parts, of even the oldest manuscripts, will enable the linguist to follow the evolution of the language.

One of the manuscripts, sent to Europe in 1748 and registered in the Bibliotheque Nationale in Paris, is the key object of this study. It tells exactly what the pronounciation was like 250 years ago and what vocabulary was used. Even more interesting, the historical manuscripts record the arrival of Arab immigrants to the Madagascar coast. They describe the problems of the first Arab settlers and their encounter with the indigenous people.

They refer to the rivalry between different groups and families and document the subsequent peace agreement which gave each clan a special role in society: such as political leadership, Islamic leadership, and responsibility for astrology and magic - they all had the task of keeping old manuscripts and recording important events. The manuscripts also give details about the invasion into Antaimoroland by a French army, under the command of Captain La Case, in the 1650s.

As the *sorabe* manuscripts represent the only written Malagasy tradition, they are of great value for the study of the history of Madagascar. However, there are evident lacunae in the presentation of Madagascar's history. There is little about the 18th century. For example, the *sorabe* does not mention that a neighbouring tribe in the 18th century elected a European, the Count Beniowsky, "King of Madagascar". It can thus be seen that the scribes limited their recording strictly to events which had a direct influence on Antaimoro life.

Rather insignificant details are also recorded, for instance, Antaimoro relations with neighbouring peoples concerning ricefields, genealogies and so on. This represents a limitation. But the tradition does give a picture of daily life. There is important information about the nation's history, especially the details concerning the Antaimoro's contact with other tribes. The manuscripts inform us about the Antaimoro relationship with inland tribes, the Antaimoro-Antananarivo agreement, their common wars against other tribes opposing their leadership.

The manuscripts left in Antananarivo by the Antaimoro delegation, some 200 years ago, form a special part of the historical manuscripts. Unfortunately the greater part of these manuscripts, which were lost and refound in 1913, were haphazardly classified and are now missing again. One hopes that these documents will be rediscovered.

In the Norwegian national archives we recently found a translation of one of the missing *sorabe* manuscripts, in the modern Malagasy alphabet, and with a Norwegian translation appended.

Accepting all the limitations, we can still speculate about the selection of events recorded. We think we have found a reason for the selectivity of events recorded in the *sorabe* tradition. By analysing one interesting *sorabe* collection of Malagasy folklore, we have noticed that only a number of selected stories have been recorded, omitting many of the most popular fairytales from the coast.

Even more interesting was the discovery that these recorded historical events, whether they were given in folklore or general narrative forms, all had a certain relation to religion. It seems as if the criterion for recording *sorabe* history is its religious, especially its astrological, interest. Only an event illuminating astrological influences on human life is considered an *interesting* event. That seems the reason why some events, despite their incontestable historical importance, are left out.

For example, the victory of Radama I over the Sakala tribe was in itself important, but the manuscript highlights the fact that the king, advised by his Anakara astrologers, started this war on a Friday - which was in a year of Friday - and under influence of a favourable *vintana* or destiny, and with the *moon* in a special favoured position.

The chronology recorded in the *sorabe* manuscripts is vague and disappointing. We have tried to compare local Malagasy chronology with that of European history, but with little success so far. The question of chronology and the lack of precision in the recording of history is a general problem for scholars studying African history.

Our analysis of the Madagascar *sorabe* manuscripts has taught us that the time and chronological expressions are primarily seen in religious terms.

THE RELIGIOUS MANUSCRIPTS

Ancestor worship was the most common religious element in the original Malagasy religion, and it is still strong in the country. But it is hardly mentioned in the *sorabe* manuscripts, apart from a few instances where they relate to the peoples' habits. That is an indication of the *sorabe's* end and object.

One also notices that references to animism, to the worship of forces in the woods and in the mountains, have been considerably reduced compared to their importance in Malagasy daily life, especially in the countryside.

However, there is another element, magic, which has been given considerably more attention. One could even say it forms the major part of the religious *sorabe* manuscripts. Certain formulae, drawings, characters or special figures are considered capable of creating, in a supernatural way, a particular situation. Connected to this is the Malagasy *sikidy* system (grains laid according to certain models), which is supposed to give the informed user knowledge and power about life and destiny.

This group, although appearing to be elementary magic thought, reveals itself, when analysed, as having connexions with Arabic astrology and it is quite different from popular magic. The already mentioned Antaimoro delegation in Antananarivo was asked several times to use their supposedly mysterious forces to create, by help of magic, formulae and powerful charms, favourable or dangerous situations. The scribes, however, rejected such demands. They considered themselves scientists and astrologers, basing their authority on scientific knowledge of the cosmos.

They were capable of predicting the future by taking into account external forces influencing human life. But they did not consider themselves sorcerers. That is why they reacted against the king's sometimes superfluous wishes to know an unessential detail, such as the colour of an unborn calf. Although they considered themselves capable of finding out such things, they thought such demands a corruption of science.

Even if this is the trend in the written *sorabe* tradition, it is apparent in Madagascar today that the *sorabe* manuscripts are used in just this primitive way as magic charms. However, this does not alter the fact that the intention of the early Arabic-Malagasy tradition was not to forward the old local religious elements (nor, perhaps, to prevent them either), but instead, to promote a general astrological Arabic tradition brought to Madagascar by the Arab immigrants. Beside the general oriental astrology brought by the Arabs, the scribes considered it their special duty to stress Koranic and other Islamic material.

In an important part of the written tradition in the *sorabe* manuscripts, we meet the *djinns*, which give an account of the appearance of birds radiating light and shadow and dispersing the smell of death, as well as having the ability of communicating with human beings. This may represent the *sorabe* contribution to the worship of the dead, in the sense that the spirit of the dead is seeking to find a relationship with a living creature. But this is not the case. These *djinn* texts do not mention burial ceremonies or propose any form of prayer or sacrifice, which has always been indispensably connected to Madagascar ancestor worship. Instead we have found that the *djinn* parts of the *sorabe* manuscripts refer to the many *djinn* verses in the Koran, with the difference being that the presentation is animated by the local religious culture. As in the Koran the Malagasy *sorabe* djinns have a certain relationship to *Rasolaiman* (Salomon) with whom they speak and discuss religious matters. Scholars working on the sufi movements in Africa with similar *djinn* doctrines, will find interesting material for comparison with Madagascar.

Despite the interest in the relationship to the Koran, there are many limitations in the religious *sorabe* manuscripts. Monotheism, which is so vital to Islamic theology, has not been sufficiently emphasized. But the manuscripts do give several interesting versions of the creation of the world, linked to the Koran's interpretation, and yet, at the same time, open to thoughts influenced by many different sources. One version is introduced with these words: *Itsy lahy naboara Zanahary masoandro asamosy, naboara Zanahary ny volana alakamary, ny vohitsy alontarida, ny taika sa tso alimareky...* (And God created the moon: alakamary, the earth: alontarida, the ocean: alimareky). Here we recognize *al sams, al quamar, al-tarid, and al-mariq.*

Finally, a note of interest about Madagascar's church history. The first Christian missionaries to Madagascar, the Lazarist fathers Naquart and Gondrée, arrived in Fort Dauphin in 1648 and in their preaching and teaching they used the name *Isa* for Jesus from the Koran. Their catechism, printed in 1657, refers to Jesus as Ryssa. (=Ra-Isa. The prefix *Ra* introduces all proper names in Madagascar). From the few Arab-Malagasy manuscripts that they gained permission to study, the missionaries learned that Jesus had already been known for centuries in Madagascar. Later, to avoid the dualistic Jesus picture of the Koran, the church found it wise to reconsider the names used in the Bible texts.

DE HOARIDE OFO NGODRI FIFITRI TARI VERETSIKITSI:
The word of God fifty-three verse six:
OLO HOI LAIKI SIPI HAVI NGONI ETSITIRIE, HOI HAVI TORONEDI
All we like sheep have gone astray, we have turned
EVERI HOANI TO IZI ONO HOIE, AD-IO LORODI HATSI LEDI
every one to his own way, and the Lord hath laid
ONI HIZI SANI DI SI SINI OFO ASI OLO
on his son the sin of us all.
ZIONI SAPITRIRA TENITSI VAIRITSI ILIEVISIN: AI AMO DI NGODRI
John chapter ten verse eleven: I am the good
SAPEERIDI. DI NGODRI SAPEERIDI NGIVITI IZI LAIFO FORO HIZI SIPI
shepherd. The good shepherd giveth his life for his sheep.
TSAMO TROE TARADI: DI LORODI IZI MAI TSEPERADI. AI SALI.
Psalm twenty-three: The Lord is my shepherd. I shall
NATRI HOANITRE. INGAILI ATATISMO.
not want. "Anglais" venant du Sud.

The Identity of Women in African Development

Marja-Liisa Swantz

INTRODUCTION

When looking at the African development process from the perspective of women, several key questions arise: Do women have an identity of their own apart from that of men within the development process? If so, is the difference between the two only one of degree of participation in development, or are there qualitative differences? If there are qualitative differences it is crucial for the development of Africa that they are detected and raised to a position from which the true proportions of women's contribution to the changing African society can be viewed without any obstacles - or at the least, issues can be freely debated without perpetuating myths and preconceived ideas which so often confuse the actual issues involved.

If women have their own identity, what prevents it from being seen more clearly and for them to have more influence in society? The question is not only how women would become more visible, but rather: How is development distorted and does the invisibility of women's identity have anything to do with the distortions? Thus, the question here is not principally how women's status could be raised and women's living conditions improved - although that too is part of the issue - but rather how development would look different if women's identity was to be more clearly recognized in it. In order to find answers to these questions the nature of development itself needs to be analysed.

THEORY AND PRACTICE OF DEVELOPMENT

During the two decades in which there has been a concerted international effort for development, especially in the so-called Third World countries, it has become evident that the lofty ideas of development proclaimed at the start of this period have had relatively little impact in terms of implementation. The major external financiers of development programmes and projects have, with verbosity, gone along with the emphasis on "the people's" development. They have even required from the recipient countries pronouncements and policies that promote an egalitarian outcome and strive towards a state in which no sectors of society are discriminated against and in which human rights are upheld. But, in practice, economic growth and cost benefit philosophy have dictated different practices, and business terms have dominated the contractual agreements.

With the rise of "basic needs" policies and strategies there has been some room for humanitarian considerations at the local level of development, but these strategies are soon forced to harness their resources to the interests of international markets. The trend is to develop trade relations based on the principle of the division of labour. Development in the Third World is conditional on the well-being of the industrial countries and their economies. From them, the Third World countries are expected to take their direction and directives. This has severe consequences for the internal development of developing countries. It touches centrally on the question of women's identity in development. The assumption that women's issues can be dealt with in a special women's sector separate from crucial economic problems is a gross distortion.

It is often assumed that if finance is provided for a few women's programmes and projects, then the "real" development business can continue on its own way, determined as it is by the economic laws of international interaction and subject to them. In the minds of dominating macro-economists alternatives can only act as deterrents. However, if development is viewed with the recognition that the development process has become distorted - that something central to it is both misconceived and misconstrued - then the question of women's identity takes on a new dimension. The question becomes: How has women's invisibility contributed to the present decline in world and in local development? What potential remedies, beyond utopian ideas, would there be? Would women plan development differently?

The development ideologies embodied in ujamaa, harambee, or in Kaunda's humanism were intended to mark the way for a different kind of development which was to serve human beings and to be achieved by their decisions and means. Instead, the development that followed has in many ways failed these ideals. Yet ideals serve as a guide; they create at least an illusion that knowledge of the terrain is available, and compasses are at hand should someone in earnest want to make use of them.

ASSUMPTIONS ABOUT WOMEN'S IDENTITY ON DEVELOPMENT

"Female Approaches" to Development

Innumerable studies have shown that women's recognized share in develop-ment has largely been in inputs of labour, while their conscious contribution to decision-making and planning has been belittled by prevailing notions about their illiteracy, ignorance and consequently their incapability of taking part in any important tasks. This has affected both women's own self-identity and male attitudes towards women in development. But beyond these firmly held views of women's incapacity there is a universal concept that *"man"* acting in development is male. Thus it has been "natural" to create develop-ment around the image of man who is male.

Ideology or strategy based on the assumption that solely economic and technological determinants decide the course of development are assumed here to carry clear marks of predominantly male values. Unless balanced by special measures in cooperation with vulnerable groups in society, such assumptions are likely to be detrimental to human development in general and to women in particular. In order to curb such developments, which can be predicted to adversely affect the environment and social and individual conditions of life, alternative ways of dealing with technological and eco-nomic change have to be found.

If female values are contrasted with male values, what here is termed the "female approach" does not mean any inherently superior female qualities derived from female biology. Rather, it is envisaged that they are the outcome of the reproductive, caring and nurturing roles that culture and biology com-bined have allotted to women. These roles have at the same time subjected women to a subservient social position in many cultures. To the extent that men can perform similar tasks, and take on similar responsibilities, a greater balance between the genders will be reached and values and attitudes will change.

Thus it is assumed here that the contemporary striving for a more just, non-violent and non-repressive world and the search for creative alternatives in development, has its roots in the social sphere, the responsibility of which has been left to women in most cultures. Even when adopted by men, they are still often identified by the society as being feminine values. On the other hand, women have adopted purely male values, and being a female does not automatically make one's approach "female". Women performing roles iden-tified as male roles adopt concomitant "male" behaviour and values.

This paper on women's identity in African development is consequently concerned first and foremost with potentially better models of development. However, improved development is possible only through a renewed understanding of women's part in development, in its actuality and potentially.

Man with a Male Identity in Development

Language does not only mirror culture, it also shapes culture. The Swahili language - like the Finnish language - does not create sex divisions, neither in its articles nor in its use of personal pronouns. Thus when a policy is written in Swahili the farmer or peasant is not automatically conceived as being male as is the case when the same text is translated into English - or when it is first perhaps even written in English. The use of English in documents and studies reaffirms that it even creates male images in relation to development policies and strategies.

A basic document of Tanzanian socialism was the Arusha Declaration, 1967. When put in English it seems to refer only to men:

> The justification of socialism is Man: not the State, nor the Flag. Socialism is not for the benefit of black men, nor brown men, nor white men, nor yellow men. The purpose of socialism is the service of man.
> (Arusha Declaration, 1967. Quoted by Bertell who stresses the bias in language, 1985, p. 14)

In discussions with men and women, both in private and in public, it has become evident that the documents on socialism were indeed conceived in terms of men's personal freedom and development, and only in political terms. This point becomes particularly clear when the TANU Guidelines, paragraph 26, has been discussed. In it, in the same way as in President Nyerere's early speeches and writings, man's development, people's development was made dependent on his personal freedom to develop himself:

> But people cannot be developed; they can only develop themselves. ... He develops himself by what he does; he develops himself by making his own decisions, by increasing his understanding by what he is doing, and why; by increasing his own knowledge and ability, and by his own full participation - as an equal - in the life of the community he lives in. ... he is not being developed if he simply carries out orders from someone better educated than himself. ... A man develops himself by joining in free discussion ... and participating in subsequent decisions; he is not being developed if he is herded like an animal ... .
> (Nyerere, *Freedom and Development*, 1973, p. 60)

Men only seldom conceive that women should have this kind of personal freedom and the right to decision-making over issues that concern them.

IDENTITY ASCRIBED TO WOMEN

There is much evidence to show that women in traditional cultures have had areas of social life in which they have dominated, and that there has been some balance between the genders. Women's ritual and nurturing roles had previously been more central within the total culture than in later periods when external influences began to affect sectors of life. Women also had a definite identity and could not be ignored or have their roles minimized. Islam, and partly also Christianity, were introduced as men's religions, and external employment and educational advancement were areas of life first limited to men. With them came social, political and economic power. The significance of the new sectors grew and areas of life which had previously been important to the whole society gradually lost their central place in social life. Women's invisibility is a result of this development. The larger the so-called "modern" sector in a society is, the further away from it and into an exclusively traditional sector the women are likely to be pushed.

Today women's self-identity is wrought with contradictions. It is shaped by the dominant value system, that of men and other "colonizers" of women and society, but it is also shaped by the social and economic reality in which women find themselves. The disregard of the real situation of women by those in authority over them has forced women out of their passive accept-ance of their position in society. The internal contradiction of the woman's situation has made her aware of the falsity of the male consciousness which she herself has unknowingly accepted in her subjected state. This explains how women in similar social situations - and even the same women on different occasions - contradict themselves. To illustrate the preceeding point, examples are taken from statements made by Bukoba Christian elders of both sexes in Bushasha village (Interviews by Magdalena Kamugisha, 3/4 1975)

Women's Identity as seen by themselves, illustrated with material from Bukoba District

A woman's value in Bukoba - and as similar cases verify, also in the

Kilimanjaro region - was judged by others and by herself by her ability to feed her family. She could not risk paying more attention to her personal cash crop except in a situation where she was otherwise hampered in her primary duty of feeding her family. A woman elder was convinced that women's main problem was economic: "the core ... is her economic dependence on men". She was divided in her opinion as to whether the economic lot of women could be improved. It would depend on the income and marketing possibilities for their *enshoro* (hard nut) cultivation. The time spent cultivating and marketing it was regulated by other factors in women's lives and their incapacity to organize transport for their produce. Another elder expressed the core of women's self-identity, which directed her consciousness: "a woman's pride is to have enough food for her family and to be happy with her husband". Women's self-identity was thus shaped by the value system which she and others accepted.

The husband was responsible for providing his own food. Yet, in his eyes her favour was dependent upon her provisions, even where he did not provide food. The conflict that occurs in such relationships creates dissatisfaction among women and an awareness of the falsity of the kind of authority where the duties accompanying such authority are not fulfilled. In that situation the acceptance of subservience has begun to crack. Because of this discrepancy, opportunities are utilized for expressing dissatisfaction.

Christian women could appropriate for themselves the freedom proclaimed in the Christian message and through this feel inwardly free. The situation was harder when women's subservience was ascribed to the authority of the Bible. "Wives be obedient to your husbands" - without an equal emphasis on the selfsacrifice for the sake of the wives ascribed in the same passage to the husbands. In comparing the situation of rural women with that of town women, a 45 year old woman emphasized the dependence on men in both cases: "Womankind has been cursed by God. We have too many problems, menstruation, child-bearing, dependency. We have nothing of our own. Not even our educated daughters ... (are in a better position). Women's curse cannot let them go freely". The woman told a story of a young wife whose entrepreneurial attitude with her husband's shop "would have made her a hero, had she been a man"; but "the world around her condemned her".

Women did not have courage to take their affairs to the magistrate, although their *de jure* position was better than their *de facto* situation. The reasons can be found in Haya culture. "They believe so much in ancestral spells". Some even travelled to Dar es Salaam to gain a court hearing, in order to be away from the influence of their surroundings. However, the male magistrate in Bukoba pointed out in 1975 that the relatively few court cases on marital problems were brought there by women.

The question arose whether the matrimonial concession in the Marriage Act of 1971 offers women any protection. It stipulates that the senior wife should give her assent before the husband, in a potentially polygamous marriage, could take another wife. The magistrate dealing with marriage cases in Bukoba pointed out that under Customary Law a man also had to ask his senior wife before taking another wife, but the speaker admitted that there were exceptions to that. However, it was the duty of the senior wife to prepare for the arrival of the junior wife. The motivation for this, as already mentioned, was the rise in status of the senior wife, and the resultant new sharing of work that accompanied this. The urban situation where the junior wife shares the relatively ease of city life, while the senior wife is left to do the work on the shamba, is the reverse of the traditional value system.

Christian women elders in Bushasha thought that broken marriages out-numbered the stable ones. The reason was said to be: "Women have seen and heard much to which they had no access before. Previously they were taught to be subject to their husbands. It kept us cool. Today you go to church, to school and to meetings and argue with men. They get 'fired' that way". It was recognized that women's status had been improved by Christianity and formal education. But, as Christians, "formerly we respected marriage more than modern women do. ... Women today are impossible".

Identity of Women as expressed by Men in Bukoba District

Men's views on this were much more outspoken. Male elders in the same village resented the idea that women should have an equal say with men. It had never been so before. Women were inferior to men and had always been so, for reasons of creation, tradition and man's superior qualities. The state-ment was defended on the grounds of three arguments: 1) Male superiority is basic in all creatures; 2) Traditionally man was the head and superior to woman; 3) Man had the courage to face reality. Another argument put forth by the Bukoba men was: Women are inferior by their status. They do not wholly belong anywhere. They belonged to no clan, either at their birthplace or at their husband's place because "there she can never acquire clan membership, no matter how long she stays there". (Interviews by M.K., April 1975, Bukoba and Bushasha)

Men blamed the wife of the then Vice-President Rashid Kawawa, who herself was the chairperson of U.W.T. and a Muslim, for trying to arouse mutiny and indiscipline among women. This was after she had run a public campaign in the streets of Dar es Salaam to oppose polygamy.

INVISIBILITY OF WOMEN IN DEVELOPMENT

In an earlier paper I have argued that a country such as Tanzania, which has witnessed a gradual decline in its agricultural production and of its economy in general, will not be able to recover unless it seriously reconsiders its policy towards women and gives conscious recognition to women's central role in production. Women do not continue to be invisible only in language but also in the remuneration of their work and in the analysis of what is wrong with development. The goal of "integrating women into development" is wrongly set as long as there is no proper analysis made of the actual costs of development projects for the economy of the country, and which sectors of the population are expected to carry the burden of those costs. Women have to pay a large part of the expense of development projects with agricultural products. Thus the real problem is how to integrate men into development, particularly into agricultural production. If this were accomplished, then perhaps also the cost of production and of development projects would be evaluated in more realistic terms. To follow up that issue is not, however, the task of this paper, as the intention is to trace the analysis of women's identity and the reasons why in many situations women remain invisible.

SOCIAL INFERIORITY LEADS TO INVISIBILITY

Are women invisible because they are so passive, take so little interest in public affairs and have no faith in themselves, as men maintain when asked why so few women are in decision-making bodies? This is not the case, as instead, invisibility is a mark of ascribed inferiority: lack of trust in the capabilities of men contributes to the women's invisibility. In this sense the peasants are "invisible" to the bureaucrats, the workers are "invisible" to the managers, and the women are "invisible" to the men. They are targets and objects, and are not expected to be creative or to contribute in any substantial way to leadership and to basic thinking. In this sense women are comparable to any subjected group in any hierarchy. On these grounds, it has been argued that women's inferiority is basically a class problem. Once there has been a reversal of hierachical order through revolutionary development, women's inferiority will also disappear. However, studies have conclusively shown that this is not the case. While the reversal of hierarchical order in society is a necessary condition for equality between men and women, it is not in itself sufficient. Thus, it would be useful to study further how women's position is different from any other subjected group.

For example, Claude Meillasoux has shown that women are a mediary group between young men and old men among the Gourou and not at the bottom of the ladder. (Meillasoux, 1981) But women, too, have to be analysed in different age groups and social strata. In the case of a polygamist group like the Gourou, or pastoralists such as the Maasai, young men compete with the older men for wives. It is in the interests of the older men to recruit the older women as their accomplices. The older women take part in the oppression of the younger women by imposing norms which benefit the interests of the older men. Similarly, amongst the Chagga the interests of the older women are in conflict with the interest of the younger women. The older generation of women has taught the younger one to obey their husbands, who are the older women's sons. This is because their sons provide their only security in old age. (Swantz, 1983, p. 85)

Similar divisions of interest follow class distinctions. It has been in the interest of a senior wife in a wealthy polygamous marriage to secure the services of the younger women, and she sees to it that the latter are subservient and obedient to her husband and thus also to her in her position of authority. This state of affairs breaks the solidarity between women - the possibility of forming a women's common front against the dominating males has been wrought with the same weaknesses as any stratified society in which dividing is a form of ruling. Although individual women may have been visible in specific circumstances, women have not been socially recognized as a gender group.

A subjected group can be treated in a way that is useful and convenient in a given situation. The dominant group dictates the terms of social intercourse and its customs and culture become natural for all concerned. But this domination may not affect all areas of common life. Its prominence depends on which sectors of life occupy the central and all invasive areas of social life. By accepting their inferior status as natural, they efface their own subcultures, which eventually become invisible.

WOMEN'S POLITICAL IDENTITY IN RELATION TO PERSONAL FREEDOM

The strong "HE" appearing in the English version of the basic political texts in Tanzania is no mere matter of language peculiarity. In the minds of the men who direct development, at the level of policy or in practice, it is taken for granted that men have a natural right to make decisions. Women's reticence in entering public life is partly explained by their personal dependence on men at each phase of their lives. Men change from the category of father or mother's brother to that of husband or son. With regard to women, socialist policies - which speak of man's right to personal freedom - are interpreted in a strictly political sense, and this excludes any rights within the social relationships of family, kin or village. As long as a woman is in a dependency relationship she is under the authority and decision-making power of the man or the category of men who under customary law are her guardians. Within these relations women cannot be thought of as having decision-making power of their own.

Today, however, women are in positions of leadership at all levels of society. It is important to isolate the conditions which led to this change in the position of women, so that local or national leaders cannot hide behind a defence of traditional culture which may no longer be operational. Norms are frequently broken and this results in new personal roles and identities, yet people in their attitudes still ascribe to women positions which no longer correspond with everyday practice. In general parlance at the national level the idea is accepted that men and women are equal and that they have the same political rights. However, when the idea is applied to a social and personal level, and when women expect the same personal rights as men (especially the right to make decisions about their own lives), the difficulty begins. Thus the concept of women's identity needs to be analysed at different levels and in different social relationships and contexts.

What needs to be shown on the one hand is that women are hampered from utilizing their full capacity for the development of their country because their freedom is restricted at crucial points. On the other hand, it is necessary also to point out that changes are happening in any case, whether men as pseudo-guardians of women want it or not. These changes are more destructive of family relationships if women encounter resistance in their efforts to manage their own and their families' lives. Obviously what is needed is a balanced consideration of all the groups who are particularly vulnerable in a period of recession.

In the domestic sphere the authority-structure has cultural connotations, defended on the basis of cultural mores. While the ideology of building the society on traditional culture still has relevance and while the women's demand for a share in decision-making and for men's participation in domestic and nurturing duties are interpreted as western feminist indoctrination, there is little hope of persuasion. A change of attitude is not achieved through debates.

Society is, however, changing and this is not always given sufficient attention. Social fermentation has destabilized marriage and large scale migration has left women with virtually sole responsibility for themselves and their children. While this means more work for women, it has allowed greater freedom and given them more opportunities. This enables women to seek remunerative employment and to manage farms instead of only doing the physical work. Statistics indicate that women head between 25 and 40 % of households in the rural areas of East Africa. The number of women who are temporarily in charge of farms is even larger as most ablebodied men in the labour recruitment areas have outside employment. The growing number of women in East African cities does not only reflect the increasing tendency of wives to accompany their husbands to town. The percentage of female divorcées and widows in the cities is considerably higher than in the countryside and this shows that women, who traditionally do not inherit land, have left the countryside in search of independent employment.

On the other hand, the case study of some villages in Bugabo area in Kagera region has shown that a considerable number of returned prostitutes have gained a position of respect in their home villages. The respect was based on their ability to acquire land and to establish themselves as independent farmers. (Swantz, 1983, p. 77) Z. Bader's study (1975, p. 33) from the same region showed that such women were accepted by other farmers and were treated as equals by their male colleagues. In an interview with a female chairperson of an ujamaa village (at that time the only female village chairperson in Tanzania), in Kilimelile, Kagera region, she thought that being a woman did not hinder her work. The village had grown. Previously it had a preponderance of women as there had been an initial input of women from Bukoba town, who had been transported with the aim of putting the urban unemployed into productive work. These women had been considered prostitutes in Bukoba. (Swantz, 1983)

The tradition of women leaders is not new as women could gain positions of authority within the chieftaincy system. In the churches women have served as elders and Christian workers. (Cf. Swantz, 1983, p. 84) Furthermore, women's authority as guardians of ancestral shrines and women as religious functionaries (waganga, walanguzi, waaguzi, wapiga ramli) were widely known and accepted. Women in such leadership positions could have men serving them, such as doing domestic duties, and they even had men servants in earlier times. In such situations, however, the classdivision is obvious. Women of a higher class could gain authority over men of a lower class, but if the woman was either on an equal social level as the man or at a lower level than him, she could not command the same authority or appropriate his services.

The basic relationship between a husband and his wife/wives is crucial to the question of women's equality. The women's potential economic independence and participation in decision-making on the domestic level are of vital importance when women's share in development is assessed in more general terms. The fact that women become heads of households is significant in this perspective, whether it is because they are abandoned by their husbands or choose to live alone in order to gain social and economic independence. My own acquaintance and discussions with women in various social situations have convinced me that women seek independence from men for the expressed purpose of not being subservient to men at the expense of their own and their children's welfare.

I draw the conclusion that the changed social situation will increasingly leave men without steady family support or even a right to their own children. In practice it will force society to change its division of labour as well as its social attitudes and social codes, and this will change the position of women in society. The question is how far a disintegration of the social fabric has to go before an awareness of the changed situation develops in either of the sexes and in the population at large. Another question is whether, when changes occur as a negative response to pressures, the women's creative potential is hampered. What positive development there is, is not the result of women's creative engagement, but rather of their strength in fighting against adverse conditions.

CONCLUDING REMARKS

What then does women's invisibility mean for today's society in Africa? It has been suggested in this paper that it is detrimental to national development when women are ignored by men at the household level, by administrators at the official level and by development and economic planners at the national and international levels. This is in spite of the increased attention paid to so-called women's issues.

Women's invisibility is not solely a matter of women's welfare, it has also led to a neglect of the working conditions of the basic labour force in agricultural production. This neglect and the conditions in which rural women continue to carry out their reproductive and productive tasks have increasingly pushed younger women out of their ascribed roles. Production is more and more in the hands of older women. New generations are creating for themselves a different identity. Operating under a false assumption of the power of tradition and ignoring the actual reality can only lead the nation to increased economic and social difficulties. For that reason, it is essential that the real situation is given recognition and the women's central role in the new situation is recognized. Women's new identity can be made a matter of national and international pride.

The paper has also tried to show that the objective conditions of life are such that if an attitudinal change does not take place and lead to widely implemented policy decisions, social disintegration will continue and result in a changing family structure, increasing weakening of the economy of the country and failed development efforts. It has also been suggested that women's greater participation in shaping development goals and strategies will lead to a more balanced development planning because of their nurturing and life sustaining roles in society.

REFERENCES

Z.K. Bader, *Women, Private Property and Production in Bukoba District*, MA Thesis, Department of Sociology, University of Dar es Salaam, 1975.

T. Bertell, "Effects of Finnish Development Cooperation on Tanzanian Women", *Tanzanian Rural Women and their Crucial Role in Development*, Report 5 B, University of Helsinki, Institute of Development Studies, 1985.

M. Kamugisha, Interviews in Bukoba and Bushasha, 1975.

C. Meillasoux, *Maidens, Meals and Money. Capitalism and the Domestic Economy*, Cambridge University Press, 1981.

J. Nyerere, *Freedom and Development*, Oxford University Press, 1973.

M-L Swantz, *Tansanian nainen* , Suomen antropologinen seura, Helsinki, 1983; also M-L Swantz, *Women in Development: Creative Role Denied*, C. Hurst & Co., 1985.

M-L Swantz, *Where does the Ignoring of Women Lead to: Constraints on Women in Tanzania*, The Scandinavian Institute of African Studies, Uppsala, 15.2.1984.

Islam, Development and African Identity: The Case of West Africa

Peter B. Clarke

GENERAL INTRODUCTION

Development and modernization are as much as anything else moral and religious issues posing major problems of meaning and identity in Africa as elsewhere. The observations and assessments in this paper are for the most part confined to West Africa but before considering the situation there it might be worthwhile looking at the problem of meaning and development elsewhere. In Japan, as Bellah states, "one very widespread response to modernization has been to see it as disturbing and disorienting - as creating an unsatisfactory situation which must be mastered and overcome".[1]

Attempts to overcome the modern, perceived as embodied in Anglo-American culture in this case, have varied from an exaltation of the "Japanese spirit" (Nihon Seishin) - "a notion compounded of primordial religio-social images focusing on the divine emperor"[2] - to a reinterpretation of Buddhism, to the resort to science and technology, especially arms, to the establishment of new religious movements in which millenialism is a prominent theme and sometimes combined with extreme right wing political attitudes, as was the case with Soka Gakkai (Value Creation Society). While some Japanese new religions of the post World War II era can best be characterised as revolutionist in terms of their response to the world, the majority it would appear are manipulationist.[3] They do not seek to undermine the values of the wider society, but rather to enable people to develop the right mental and emotional attitudes so that they can cope with the demands made by that society and succeed in it without experiencing disorientation, alienation and loss of identity. In contemporary Japan, moreover, the aim of many new religions such as Sekai Kyusei Kyo (Church of

World Messianity) is to inject a spirit of community and religion into the work place, into technology into "modern" life as a whole.

In Indonesia,[4] in Iran, in Egypt and in many other developing countries outside West Africa we find the same or a similar response to what are regarded as the degenerative and destructive influences of the modern, which is seen as having reduced the "traditional" cosmologies of these societies to the realm of superstition and fantasy. It was this that promted Seyyed Hossein Nasr to write *An Introduction to Islamic Cosmological Doctrines*. In it he states:

> The Muslim world until now has had no need to be conscious of the cosmos in which it has lived. But now faced with the challenges of the modern sciences which are the fruit of a totally different conception of the modern world, the Muslims must bring into light the Islamic conception of the cosmos if they are to avoid the dangerous dichotomy which results from the superficial "harmony" between the Islamic perspective and the modern sciences to be seen so often in the writings of modern Muslim apologists. If the modern sciences are going to be anything more than an artificial "tail" grafted upon the body of Islam or even an alien element ... the Muslims must find the universal Islamic criteria in the light of which the validity of all the sciences must be judged.[5]

If they do not find these criteria then, Nasr believes, Islam will perish.

Development and modernization whatever material benefits they may bring with them in the medical and other spheres are seen as posing a direct threat to the identity of whole societies and individuals. With the introduction of modern science, technology, Western models of education and social change comes a different way of thinking and acting, a different way of life which some like Hassan al Banna, founder of the fundamentalist Muslim Brotherhood (Ikhwan) in Egypt deplore. He wrote in his memoirs:

> After the last war (World War I) and during this period which I spent in Cairo, there was an increase in spiritual and ideological disintegration in the name of intellectual freedom. There was a deterioration of behaviour, morals and deeds, in the name of individual freedom ... Books, newspapers and magazines appeared whose only aim was to weaken or destroy the influence of any religion on the masses ... Young men were lost and the educated were in a state of doubt and confusion.[6]

These few random examples of opposition to development and modernization from outside West Africa could be multiplied a thousand fold. They are not, it would seem, simply protests against the negative influence of Western attitudes on the moral behaviour of individuals and society as a whole. They are much more than that: they represent a different approach to and idea of change. While in the West the idea that conscious, directional change is primarily a human responsibility is widespread, this presents considerable problems in societies such as the ones mentioned above, and in West Africa, where the desire and need for stability of orientation, for community and continuity, in other words for identity, are necessary prerequisites for action of any sort. Moreover, there is the realization in many societies undergoing development along Western lines that not having the will or the capacity to absorb many of the changes introduced or insisted upon the inevitable result will be at best stagnation and at worst breakdown.

THE WEST AFRICAN SETTING

In Senegal, Nigeria and elsewhere in West Africa there has been a great deal of opposition to among other things the disintegrating, alienating consequences of Western models and conceptions of progress and development whether advanced by Europeans themselves or African leaders. In Mamadou Dia's view one finds the same Western notions of progress and development even in the "new" anti-colonial society of the post-independence era. In Nkrumah's socialism, he writes, one can see a Western conception of progress that is a "progrès ambiqu, partiel", and "la même image de l'homme ambivalent, la suprematie de l'objet, du technologie, la mystique de la quantité imposant à nos consciences de néophytes de cette religion nouvelle 'la force determinante des caractères statistiques bruts' (Valéry)".[7]

of Nkrumah or Sekou Touré one finds, according to Dia, little that is authentically African. Nkrumah's materialist philosophy of African socialism was not African for "the exaltation of matter and quantity is perhaps revolutionary but it is not African because devoid of any metaphysical dimension".[8] The point is that an ideology of change and progress to succeed and gain support must not only guarantee greater equality, economic wellbeing, and independence but also at the same time preserve and sustain African identity and culture.

An increasing number of Muslims are prepared to argue that Islam alone can offer a political and economic model of development which at the same time will ensure genuine progress in all spheres of life while safeguarding African identity. There is a long list of observers and participants in the West African situation, both African and European, who have suggested that Islam is more African than Christianity meaning that it has adapted itself better to the African mentality and condition.[9] I will cite just one of these,

Professor Robin Horton. With reference ro recent history in Africa Horton wrote: "Islam seems to have been fairly tolerant of its catalytic role. It has been tolerant in allowing the individual to make his own particular selection from official doctrines ... added to all this it has never itself renounced a concern with the explanation, prediction and control of space time events. Hence ... It has been able to expand without throwing off a shower of doctrinally dissenting breakaway sects".[10] All of this contrasts with the rigid, dogmatic, world rejecting approach of Christianity.[11] We will return to this thesis in the concluding section of this paper.

Considering the relevance of Islam to the African condition more from a political and economic perspective, Mazrui maintains that its relatively equalitarian, communalistic and anti-cumulative dimensions make it highly compatible with 20th century modernism which has a strong communalistic and welfarist character.[12] Moreover while Christianity, especially in its Protestant form, is said to promote a degree of individualism which militates against democratic centralism and/or a one party state, Islam may well create the more favourable conditions for this given its combination of egalitarianism and authoritarianism.[13] Furthermore, Islam is seen as part of the explanation for much of the cultural defensiveness against the West found in the late Sekou Touré's Guinea and elsewhere, and for "the selfconscious and defiant sense of community that exists in many Muslim countries in Africa". Christianity by way of contrast is seen as having inculcated the "soft" virtues of gentleness and submission creating in Africans an inferiority complex.[14]

In Sekou Touré's Guinea Islam was made to stand for what the President believed it ought to stand for and, as in Tanzania, it was only allowed to influence policy making to the extent that it was prepared to endorse and legitimate the methods and objectives set by the State for the progress and development of the country.[15]

In West Africa today it is not uncommon to hear Muslims speak insistently of the benefits to be derived by the nation as a whole from the establishment of an Islamic state, and the implementation of Islamic social and economic policies. But the question poses itself: to what extent is Islamic socialism compatible with the kind of socialist policies envisaged by the leadership and the political theorists mentioned above? While proponents of Islamic socialism and democracy like the Senegalese Cheikh Touré may share some of the goals of scientific socialism they clearly do not endorse the scientific theory of historical materialism or the view that "man is a product of society" and that "the people are the beginning and the end of everything".[16]

Islamic socialists are essentially idealist in their interpretation of material improvement and the sovereignty of the people, emphasising that both are the consequences of the proper observance of God's law and attributable to Him alone. Like Cheikh Touré of Senegal influential Muslim spokesmen in Nigeria such as Alhaji Gummi, former Grand Qadi of northern Nigeria, while believing that Islam has the answer to the problems of contemporary society, they would reject scientific socialism both as a philosophy and instrument of national policy.

However, there is some evidence to suggest that, in the Nigerian context at least, Islam furthers the growth of class consciousness principally by providing a language for politico-religious discourse. In the case of Karno factory workers, for example, worker militancy expressed in strike action seems to be higher among members of the Muslim brotherhoods and among those who have received an Islamic education than among others.[17]

For such workers, a fundamentalist rejection of Western, "Christian" institutions contained in a popular Islamic "nationalism" is carried over into the factory. A rejection of "foreign ways and exploitation" there becomes more precisely defined as a rejection of "the injustices of the capitalist system". This experience creates support not only for Islamic fundamentalism but also for those political and organisational instruments that are available to eradicate class distinctions based on ownership and control of the means of production.[18] Thus, amongst the small Kano proletariat, fundamentalism appears tinged strongly with socialist themes, and "exploitation" takes on the character of the principal enemy. It seems likely that such Muslims will "discover" within Islam further themes which will permit their religion to act as a vehicle for nascent class consciousness.

To what extent "Islamic socialism" could become a viable ideology for Nigeria remains, obviously, to be seen. There are, as we have seen, many educators and politicians in Nigeria, and in Africa, ready to emphasise the similarities between what is called "African socialism" and Islamic socialism. They suggest that a sense of communal solidarity and the collective ownership of land are to be found in both socialisms, and resist ideas of class struggle. Utopian projections in the past present early Islamic, and pre-colonial African society as essentially classless, collective and communal. Class division is seen as the product of colonialism and imperialism, and will disappear when these forces are eradicated.

However little historical justification there is for such theories and the equivalence between the two socialisms, their role is ideological. Political leaders propounding these views seek to legitimise their programme of change, and hope to unite and integrate their countries. Bringing together the value-laden terms "Islamic", "African" and "Socialist", such legitimation hopes to capture the major ideological symbols of the modern African state. Conversely it places its proponents outside the damaging ideological sphere of the "Western, capitalist, neo-colonialism", the "Godless" and the "Eastern bloc". It offers a *via media* between the world's two conflicting political ideologies, both of which are readily denounced using the ultimate nationalist pejorative, ... "foreign". More important, it affords a degree of intellectual and cultural independence which strict adherence to the principles of Western capitalism or scientific socialism appears to negate.

Such an equation between Islamic and African socialism for many influential Muslims would, though, be meaningless. They would argue that a just and egalitarian society can only be established on firm Islamic foundations. Furthermore, a Muslim, they maintain, can have no dealings with, or accept, any compromise, in any form, with other religions and ideologies.[19] Neither would such "fundamentalists" seek the kind of unity that destroys diversity, nor find the label "African" particulary meritorious. Their objectives would be the integration of the *umma* rather than the nation-state. They would share with the majority of Nigerian Muslims the belief that social justice came through the correct application of Shari'a law, rather than through African or Marxist praxis. We can turn for a moment to the question of the nation state and the Islamic fundamentalist view of its relevance.

ISLAMIC FUNDAMENTALISM AND THE NATION-STATE; NIGERIA AND SENEGAL

Nigeria

In Nigeria, in recent years, there have been a number of occasions on which Muslims have refused to recite the national pledge or the national anthem, claiming that to do so would be against the teachings of Islam.[20] They represent a small minority of Muslims who consciously reject the idea of the nation-state and whose primary objective is not Nigerian unity and stability but the unity of all Muslims. The position is to be contrasted with that of the majority who see their role as "facilitating the good government of Nigeria".[21] The constitution for such Muslims is viewed as a "fundamental treaty" binding upon Muslims insofar as it is compatible with Islam. Even amongst fundamentalists who criticise the present constitution and seek an

Islamic state, they recognise that a Nigerian state based on the principles of the Qur'an and Sunna alone is unattainable "given the present realities of the country".[22] They seek not the elimination of the nation-state but one run on Islamic lines and achieved by democratic means.

The model of the Islamic "nation" posited by moderate fundamentalists is the community established by the Prophet Muhammad at Medina.[23] Moreover, they emphasise the relevance of the Medina constitution for Nigeria in its attempt to achieve communal integration, "to create a unified political community out of diverse peoples".[24] The content of this model must, however, be "the intrinsic values sustaining the social organisation of a Muslim community".[25] Apart from the all-important Shari'a, these are "the principle of consultation" i.e. "democratic elections, free speech and freedom of the Press", a "brotherly spirit", the "moral tone of the community" and "welfarism" or "the broad Islamic concept of charity (Zakat)".[26]

The moderate fundamentalists who fully accept that the world Muslim community cannot exist as a single entity were seen by some opponents as the National Party of Nigeria (N.P.N.) at prayer. Many non-Muslims feared that once the N.P.N. came to power the constitution would be modified, non-Muslims in the party would be shown to be window-dressing, and a major attempt to impose Islam nationally would take place. That this did not take place demonstrated the degree of misunderstanding of the Nigerian political parties shown by those who saw them as mere epiphenomena of religious blocs rather than diverse interest groups. Far from any predicted merger between the predominantly northern based and predominantly Muslim political parties, the N.P.N., P.R.P. and the G.N.P.P. (Greater Nigeria Peoples' Party), it was the "Christian" Nigeria Peoples' Party, N.P.P. that forged an alliance with the ruling N.P.N. The alliances of the political parties expressed underlying socio-economic realities and expedience, as well as simple regional arithmetic.

The voting patterns of the 1979 elections demonstrated clearly that Nigerians vote more along regional, or ethnic, lines than according to religion. Christians in the Middle Belt, the east and south-east of the country and in Rivers State voted in relatively large numbers for the N.P.N. On the other hand Muslims in the western states, and even in Gongola State in the north, voted for the Unity Party of Nigeria (U.P.N.) led by Chief Awolowo.[27] Voting behaviour in the north and south has been traditionally different, with the north showing a stronger regional identity. The old Northern Peoples' Congress (N.P.C.) used the slogan "One north, One People, irrespective of religion, race or tribe" to considerable effect. This enabled the predominantly Hausa-Fulani party to obtain an overall majority in the first Federal Parliament, which collapsed in the military coup of January 1966.[28] With the exception of the Christian Middle Belt peoples, particularly the Idoma, recruited to the N.P.C. banner, Islam probably provided a unifying force in sustaining regional identity in this period.

The weakness of religion as a dominant criterion determining political preference in Nigeria today demonstrates the limits of Islamic fundamentalism. For the majority, pan-Islamic hopes are utopian and to be rejected. But if the Medinan model of Islamic society is to be created by democratic methods, either nationally, or at the level of predominantly Muslim states like Sokoto state, the realities of electoral politics have to be taken into account. To win a majority for its presidential candidate, and in the national assembly, under the present suspended constitution, a predominantly Muslim-controlled party like the N.P.N. needed support from non-Muslims troughout the Federation. For such support to be forthcoming from non-Muslims, the dominant party had to show a convincing emancipation from sectarian religious objectives. A Party that endorsed a drive for "authentic" Islamic states within the Nigerian Federation could not have hoped to retain such support. In short, Nigeria has gone too far along the path of integration at the political, economic, communications, educational, and to some extent cultural level, for the creation of "states within the State" to be electorally acceptable. This integration, learnt and cherished at the appalling cost of the Nigerian civil war, is unlikely to yield before the tide of Islamic fundamentalism.

Senegal

In Senegal the goal of the creation of an Islamic state dominates all the activity of Muslims like Cheikh Touré of Dakar. In his Muslim monthly journal *Etudes Islamiques* and the Press, the fundamental principles governing an Islamic state are debated in a way not found in Nigeria. Moreover this forms part of a "campaign of enlightenment" conducted in order to win over youth, the leaders of the brother-hoods, and marabouts, to the creation of an Islamic Republic. In January 1981 Muslims were pursuing a major political drive to establish Islamic knowledge and Arabic as subjects taught in all state schools. For Senegalese Muslims like Touré the Islamic state was the only form of state in which "the universal rights of man, and the existence of universal man are recognised".[29]

The openness of Senegalese integralism to overtly political goals cannot be attributed to propitious local conditions. No viable coalition between the leading marabouts of the major brotherhoods, the Tijaniyya and Muridiyya, and youth, exists nor is it likely to occur for a very long time. From the integralist perspective, the leading marabouts have been mentally colonised by the French into an apolitical and "purely" religious role. Though the grand marabouts undoubtedly influence Senegalese politics they do so indirectly and informally, showing little inclination to support publicly calls for an Islamic Rebublic.

The silence of the majority of marabouts on the central goal of the integralists has been eloquent during the last four years. In November 1979, Abdullah Niass proclaimed a Senegalese "Islamic Republic" in Paris, allegedly supported by Libya. He was arrested in April 1981. After two years his party *Hizbullahi* (the Party of God) had gained very little support in Senegal and his arrest caused very little concern or upset. Tellingly his "uncle", a Grand Marabout of the Ibrahim Niass branch of the Tijaniyya, and a successor to Ibrahim Niass, went on record that "though Muslims might like or desire an Islamic state this was not a viable proposition at the present time in Senegal".[30]

To date no Islamic Party has successfully been formed in Senegal though a demand for one was made during Leopold Senghor's term of office and rejected. Not long after his retirement in December 1980, a further application for registration was made at the Ministry of the Interior by the "Rally for National Salvation", a Party "inspired in its activities by the principles of Islam". Since political parties in Senegal, as in Nigeria, are not allowed to be identified with sect, race, religion, ethnic group or regional language, the registration was rejected. Despite the indisputable influence of the Ayatollah Khomeini in Senegal, no recognisably Islamic Party amongst the thirteen registered for the Presidential and National Assembly elections of March 1983 was recognised.

The integralist response has been to inform their Muslim co-religionists that acceptance by them of non-Islamic political, legal, educational and moral systems was tantamount to apostasy, to rejecting Islam in favour of another system of belief and practice.[31] Touré himself went so far as to advocate jihad in the manner of al hajj Umar Taal for the purpose of protecting the Islamic faith and the cultural heritage of Senegal. His vision of Senegal's future is one in which an inevitable process of westernization accompanied by secularization will destroy all that is "authentically" Senegalese, by which he means Islamic.[32]

In attacking "secularism" the integralists are attacking as much as anything else what they see as the subtle marginalization of Muslims already reduced, as they see it, to a sort of dhimmi status in what is a predominantly Muslim country. And why the Iranian Revolution appealed so much to Touré and his associates was on account of the fact that it destroyed in practice the distinction in socio-political affairs between the public sector and religion as a private concern. It is this distinction regarded as fundamental to the secular state principle which, according to Touré, while assuring Muslims as individuals a modicum of toleration, at the same time suppresses the cultural and moral factors pertaining to the Islamic community (umma) and on which full participation in society depends.

Iran was also important for Touré in that it provided him with the only example in modern history of genuine democracy (dimugratiyya) and socialism (ishtirakiyya). Western forms of democracy which the integralists in Nigeria are prepared to tolerate are in Touré's view the product of necessity. "Two world wars", he states "were necessary and a whole set of economic and political constraints before women were given recognition and then only hypocritically".[33] It is the same charade that the French bequeathed to Senegal. By way of contrast Islamic democracy is grounded in the divinely ordained sovereignty of the people as a whole.

This line of argument and the strong emphasis placed on Islam as a viable alternative to existing political and socio-economic systems in both Nigeria and Senegal, and the readiness to have it measured by its capacity to deal with the problems of underdevelopment and "modernization", carries with it paradoxically the strong possibility of relativising Islam, turning it into but another ideological option.

THE APPEAL OF ISLAM IN WEST AFRICA

Islam in recent times has perhaps made the most rapid progress in West Africa, in Nigeria, Upper Volta and Ivory Coast, the last two countries being regarded at the beginning of the twentieth century as "non-Muslim" by the colonial administration. During the 1960s a random sample of people in Upper Volta, both Muslim and Christian, were agreed that Islam had been making progress and some 72% believed that it would continue.[34] Amongst the reasons given were Islam's effective use of radio, the feeling that it was an "African" religion, and that it was easier to become, for example, a Muslim than a Catholic Christian.

The process in Upper Volta appears to have been a continuous one throughout the colonial period. In Wagadugu *province* at the turn of the century there were some 7 000 Muslims out of a total population of 300 000.

By 1956 an estimated 32% of Wagadugu town's half million population was Muslim.[35] At independence between 800 000 and one million of Upper Volta's population, c. 25% were Muslims.[36] This steady increase was largely due to the role of the brotherhoods, particulary the Hammalliyya branch of the Tijaniyya and the Qadariyya. The key agents of conversion had been Dyula traders and dynamic, charismatic figures like marabout Iya Haidara from Kankan in Guinea (Conakry).

Like most of the West African territories, the southern part of the Ivory Coast was categorised as non-Muslim by the French authorities. Though there were some long-standing Muslim communities in the north, very few Muslims lived in the south by 1900. But by the beginning of World War II, one historian points out with some exaggeration, "an Islamic Ivory Coast was a reality".[37] The percentage of Muslims in the overall population had risen from 7% in 1921 to 22% at independence in 1960.[38]

Again, Dyula traders and marabouts were probably the major agents of Islamisation. By the 1920s, the Dyula who were trusted and admired by the French, were established in all the important commercial centres and at strategic points on the trade routes crossing Ivory Coast. Wherever they settled, Qur'anic schools were started and the beginnings of an Islamic society put in place. Marabouts from the north attempted to win over chiefs and wealthy village leaders, registering mass conversions in some villages even before the First World War.[39]

While the complex processes at work in conversion to Islam in Nigeria doubtless were also in play, membership of the Muslim community in Ivory Coast and Upper Volta had a strong element of political opposition to westernization and colonialism. Moreover, Islam today is seen by some as the major force opposed to neo-colonialism, providing order and stability in a rapidly changing, insecure world made even more uncertain by the "irrational" workings of the capitalist system.[40]

In the territories considered more as Islamic in the colonial period, for example in Senegal, progress has also been made recently. The more rapid spread of Islam in recent years in some regions, like Haute-Casamane, has been attributed to a number of factors: declining French influence, improved communications and transport enabling marabouts to travel more freely and creating possibilities for mixing between Muslims and non-Muslims.[41] Implicit in such judgements about Islam's progress is the African feeling that Islam represents a viable alternative to the West, a religion that defines its adherents as culturally African nationalist.

AFRICAN CONVERSION TO ISLAM: THEORETICAL PROBLEMS

The rise of Islam in West Africa, and its continued success after the close of the colonial period, has stimulated a number of different causal explanations. Perhaps one of the most debated and fashionable today is that of the anthropologist Robin Horton, already mentioned, whose research field was Nigeria. At the expense of reducing and oversimplifying his theory, it amounts to the hypothesis that the monotheistic religions, Islam and Christianity, expanded and succeeded because they answered needs that had arisen within Africa's traditional religious systems. They were "catalysts for changes that were in the air anyway".[42]

In essence Horton argues that a "basic" African cosmology exists which has a two-tier structure: the first, or "lower" tier is that of the lesser spirits, the second or higher tier that of the Supreme Being. The role of the lesser spirits is to "underpin events and processes in the microcosm of the local community and its environment", while that of the Supreme Being is to perform the same function within the wider world, the macrocosm. Since there were interactions between microcosm and macrocosm, the lesser spirits were understood to be "manifestations of the Supreme Being or as entities ultimately deriving their power from him".[43] With the opening up of the microcosm through frequent and more systematic relationships with the macrocosm, the role and importance of the Supreme Being within the religious system would grow. Enter Islam and Christianity.

Christianity and Islam would be adopted, therefore, as an elaboration of understanding about the nature of the Supreme Being in those cosmologies in which this was possible. The crucial variables in African responses to these religions are "the pre-existing thought patterns and values, and the pre-existing socio-economic matrix" of individual societies.[44] The object of study should not be Islam and Christianity in Africa but rather "the development of that which was inherent in the traditional religions",[45] not the credal formulas, rituals and ethics of the world religions, but the local primal religions and their Supreme Beings. In this sense the role of agents of Islamisation, and missionaries, are secondary to the dynamics of the local religious system and its responses to changing conditions and the modern world.

The logic of this "intellectualist" argument is that neither Christian nor Muslim missionaries have changed African beliefs and practices in a profound way. Their religion has merely harmonised, or failed to harmonise, with responses of the pre-existing religious system to the modern world. To quote Horton: "where such beliefs and practices have no counterpart in these responses they tend to be weakly developed or absent from the life of the converts ... (and) where responses of the traditional cosmology to other factors of the modern situation have no counterparts in the beliefs and practices of the world religions, they tend to appear as embarrassing additions to the life of the convert".[46]

Horton is thus able to provide an *a priori* assessment of the relative success of Islam and Christianity. With modernisation their success is assured, Islam more so than Christianity because of its "this-worldly" character being seen as most appropriate to modern life. Furthermore as we have seen Islam does not, at least in practice, reject the most valuable elements of traditional African cosmologies, their predictive, explanatory and controlling dimensions in everyday life, and Islam will benefit from this tolerance. This reworking of the "syncretist" account of Islam compares Islam to the doctrinally orthodox Christianity which creates independent African Churches in which traditional cosmological concerns are more fully expressed. In short, Islam as we mentioned already is more prepared to accept a humble role as catalyst and a wide range of levels of commitment; "it does not nag excessively at those who lie towards the pagan end of the continuum".[47]

This intellectualist theory is essentially Durkheimian: primitive religions are treated as cosmologies with structural correspondences between symbolic classifications and social organisation. The classifications, to quote Durkheim, aim "to make intelligible the relations which exist between things ... to correct ideas, to unify knowledge".[48] A causal relationship exists between the social order and the conceptual order, a relationship that is assumed rather than proved.[49] Similarly, implicit in this theory is an evolutionary sequence towards "higher" i.e. scientific thought, or, in Horton's thinking, towards monotheistic cults.

Not surprisingly Horton has been strongly criticised both at a theoretical and empirical level. Fisher has called in question the alleged dynamism of traditional religious systems suggesting that Christianity and Islam, carriers of literacy and a universalist ideology are causes rather than catalysts of change.[50] Equally, Horton's evolutionary sequence is not borne out by case studies. Dramatic changes in the microcosm, opening it up in the colonial period to world trade and the "macrocosm", has produced as much belief in witchcraft, spirit possession, traditional ritual and worship as, arguably, in a Supreme Being. Societies which have been little touched by the modern world have, conversely, developed strong High God cults.

Indeed "microcosm" and "macrocosm" are sufficiently vague to be applied to many different levels of social interaction.

Though Horton's theory is at a level of generalisation that admits many pieces of contrary evidence, it has had the advantage of directing attention at local religious systems. To date this has been more illuminating in the case of Christianity's penetration of African societies, than for Islam where Islamicists have often adopted a normative approach that prescinds from local adaptations. Where the intellectualist hypothesis is most unhelpful is in the treatment of fundamentalist responses to the world religions in Africa, which have a growing importance. The radical rejection of key aspects of African religious themes, prediction, explanation, control, seen in the re-form and fundamentalist tradition of Islam have, at least historically, been the most dramatic manifestations of Islam in Africa.

Islamic attempts to answer these needs within an Islamic framework have certainly characterised some of these movements. However, the last thing that has marked them is converts identifying the "significant equivalences", the "elective affinities" between his/her old religious system and the new Islamic system, as Horton would have it. The significance of the move-ments has been a desire to break entirely with the pagan past, a motivation found also in Bible-centred Christian sects in Africa. It might be argued that African conversion to the world religions depends on converts' appreciation of the difference between their new and old religions, rather than the similarities, whether at a conscious or Durkheimian unconscious level. Though no-one would seriously doubt that religious belief exists as part of a continuum of different forms of understanding the world, Horton fails to explain the purifying dynamic, that moves towards a totalisation of explanation in Islamic categories and characterises the fundamentalist spirit. It is this dynamic, found in Christian fundamentalism, and organisationally, in monasticism, that is expressed at different intensities in the two world religions, and may be the most important parameter in analysing their method of expansion.

Another theory which initially appears plausible on the basis of case studies is the "Market Value" theory of Islamic expansion, along the lines of Tawney and Weber's treatment of Protestantism. The ethic of Islam, it is claimed, is a secular, market/commerce oriented ethic, see Qur'an, Sura 198. The alliance of market and mosque permitted Islam's phenomenal expansion in West Africa. This does not, of course, explain either why some communities unassociated with trading converted to Islam nor why many traders and businessmen did not. Above all, it overlooks the role of malams and education. In the Senegambia, for example, in some areas, marabouts succeeded where traders and *jihads* had failed.[51]

The Muslim cleric as healer, diviner, provider of amulets as well as educator of youth was crucial to the spread of Islam in Africa. African needs for prediction, explanation and control came via the malam, not as syncretism, but in Arabic literacy. Shar'ia law as well as in *sihr*, Islamic magic, Qur'anic verses dipped in water which is drunk, and in the range of the arts of the rural wandering malam. Such individuals represented a religious cornucopia, offering a package to satisfy religious need, and initiated people and communities into a wider Islamic community, which happened often to find its major form of cohesion in clientship and trade. Islam was adapted to the trading world of West Africa not because of its internal ethic, which can be, and is interpreted in a variety of ways, but because of the Muslim control of trade in the *bilad-al-Sudan*. In the same way bankers and businessmen in Europe become freemasons, not because of its capitalist ethic, but because of its commercial network and mutual help.

ISLAM: THE RELIGION OF AFRICA?

Implicit in much discussion about conversion to Islam is, as we have seen, the often expressed belief that Islam, in contrast to Christianity, is an "African religion". That is why Africans are attracted to it. At times this has paternalistic connotations. Islam demands less of Africans than Christianity, it is claimed. A total break with the past is not required and up to four wives are permissible. Conversely, the Christian African is supposed to be "schizophrenic"; colonial stereotypes abound with, ironically, even Nigerian pastors and professors taking them to heart, believing that Christianity was "imposed", Islam "organic", Churches, alien, Mosques, indigenous.[52]

The positivist element in these views amounts to the idea that Christianity contains "higher", more difficult metaphysical truths and more demanding moral codes than Islam. "Now conscience when conditioned by Christianity is an exceedingly difficult thing for a trader (African) to manage satisfactorily for himself. A mass of compromises have to be made with the world and the man who is always making compromises gets either sick of the thing that keeps on nagging at him about them or he becomes merely gaseous-minded all round ...", wrote Mary Kingsley. In contrast, Islam gave a clearer "line of rectitude ... under African conditions".[53]

Positivism, refracted through popular European thought, has in reality created a set of myths and propositions that lie behind most explanations of Islamic expansion in Africa. They lie behind both the theory of "Market Value" and Horton's intellectualist theories, and have become virtually self-confirmatory and self-justifying. There is no hard evidence that Africans who wanted to turn to trade found in Islam a set of beliefs, language, and ethic more appropriate than that available in Christianity, except in the trivial sense that in some areas most traders were Muslims. The supposed "fit" with African family patterns is equally suspect. Recent research in Ife division of western Nigeria shows that through economic pressures, education and Christianity, polygyny will soon be "a rarity"; this does not appear to have influenced Islam's progress in the region.[54]

Under the conditions of West Africa's economic dependence on the Western world, and the links of its national elites with the West, positing Islam as an "African religion" has obvious ideological significance. Some Muslims collaborated to their short-term benefit with colonialism, just as some Muslim leaders today support a neo-colonialist dispensation and social systems based on wealth and privilege in which injustice and inequality is striking. The rhetoric of Islamic brotherhood and community has been used to good effect to deflect attention from social policies that are opening up an ever greater gulf between a wealthy minority of Muslims and the mass of the rural poor in the Muslim community.

However, the effects of this rhetoric and the hopes of some African socialists that Islam contains some inherent immunity to capitalism, have contributed to giving conversion to Islam a broader socio-political dimension and this is viewed more favourably than that of Christianity. Coupled with its non-Western cultural elements and its openness to many religious needs that were eliminated in the secularism of Western European Christianity, Islam shows a small but distinct advantage over institutional Christianity in the 1980s in West Africa.

However the outbreaks of new prophetic sects growing out of Islam, like the Maitatsine sect now banned by the Nigerian government, indicate that mainstream Islam will be judged by the poor just as ruthlessly as the failing political systems against which it has featured so favourably in the last decade.

CONCLUSIONS

The extraordinary variety of peoples and communities, with different occupations and needs, that have converted to Islam this century in West Africa illustrate the impossibility of finding any monocausal explanation for Islam's appeal.

The content of Islam, unfiltered through the alien soil of liberalism, secularism and the technological world through which Christianity had passed before it reached West Africa as a missionary religion, was perhaps a richer food for spiritual need in West Africa. Possibly more of the convert's religious needs were answered, and answered in a way that did not erect two worlds, one of a private religious kind, one of a public secular kind. Moreover, Islam offered converts concrete new personal relationships and a living community that was not apart from his/her everyday socio-economic life.

One of the needs which was instrumental in bringing conversion, as Horton emphasises, was for a belief system and language which made sense of the rapidly changing world of post-independence countries, changes that were often perceived after an initial enthusiasm as decline and "things falling apart". Both the world religions, in a sense, competed with rival explanations, their success depending in large measure not so much on their intellectual content as the effectiveness of the evangelising, proselytising agents. In the final analysis people converted to Islam because they saw Islam as recognisable people in community, with beliefs they could accept, rituals they admired, an education they aspired to, and involving a transition that was not too abrupt compared to the benefits that would accrue when it had been completed.

The context of modern West Africa will doubtless continue to favour for the immediate future a movement of peoples from primal to monotheistic religions. Both Christianity and Islam will be fishing in the same pool. The magnified effects of the collapsing world economic order in the region will surely evoke salvationist elements within African religious consciousness, pitting "Jesus saves" against eschatological themes in Islam with their utopian projections into the future as alternative hopes and explanations. The outstanding issue remains not so much which of the world religions is the more African in principle but how these religions are interpreted, what cultural form they take, and what effect they have on the convert's relationship to the modern world of West Africa.

142

NOTES

1. R.N. Bellah, Meaning and Modernization, *Religious Studies*, Vol. 4, No. 1, October 1968, pp. 37-45.
2. Ibid.
3. B.R. Wilson, *Religious Sects*, London, 1970.
4. C. Geertz, *Islam Observed*, Chicago, 1968.
5. S.H. Nasr, *An Introduction to Islamic Cosmological Doctrines* (Revised edition), London, 1978, p. 22.
6. Citation from C. Phelps Harris, *Nationalism and Revolution in Egypt*, The Hague, 1964, p. 146.
7. M. Dia, *Islam et Civilizations Negro-Africaines*, Dakar-Abidjan-Lome, 1980, p. 92.
8. Ibid., p. 93.
9. For same examples see P.B. Clarke, *West Africa and Islam, A Study of Religious Development from the 8th to the 20th Century*, London, 1982, chaps. 7 and 8.
10. R. Horton, African Conversion, *Africa*, Vol. 41, No 2, April 1971, pp. 85-108, p. 105.
11. Ibid.
12. A.A. Mazrui, *Political Values and the Educated Class in Africa*, London, 1978, p. 143.
13. Ibid., p. 148.
14. Ibid., p. 151.
15. Ahmed Sekou Touré, *Islam for the People's benefit*, Conakry, 1977. On the question of Islam and Socialism in Contemporary Africa see D. Westerlund, *From Socialism to Islam?* Research Report No 61, Scandinavian Institute of African Studies, 1982.
16. Touré, ibid., p.17.
17. P. Lubeck, "Conscience de Classe et Nationalisme Islamique à Kano", *Politique Africaine*, 1, 4, November 1981.
18. Ibid.
19. Alhaji Gummi, *New Nigerian*, 11 May 1978, p. 5.
20. *West Africa* 1 June 1981, p. 1257. Also interviews - Sokoto, Zaria, Kaduna, October 1980, August-September 1981, April 1982.
21. Lateef Adegbite, "The Role of Muslim Leaders in contemporary Nigeria" (unpublished paper), 1978, p. 4.
22. Ibid.
23. Ibid., "The Islamic way of Nation Building", *Orita*, Vol. 8, No. 2, December 1974, pp. 106-114.
24. Ibid., p. 107.
25. Ibid.
26. Ibid., p. 110.
27. O. Oyediran, *The Nigerian 1979 Elections*, London, 1981.
28. M. Peil, *Nigerian Politics. The People's View*, London, 1976, p. 75.
29. Interviews, Dakar, April 1981.
30. Interviews, Kaolack, April 1981.
31. *Etudes Islamiques*, March 1980.
32. Ibid.
33. Ibid.

34. R. Deniel, "Croyances Religieuses et Vie Quotidienne. Islam et Christianisme à Ouagadougou", *Recherches Voltaiques*, Ouagadougou, 1970, p. 121.
35. Clarke, *West Africa and Islam*, op. cit., pp. 212-215.
36. Ibid.
37. J.L. Triavel, "La Question Musulmane en Cote d'Ivoire (1893-1939)", *Revue Française d'Histoire d'Outre Mer*, No. 61, 1974, p.546.
38. Clarke, *West Africa and Islam*, op. cit., p. 215.
39. Ibid., p. 216.
40. A. Touré, *La Civilization Quotidienne en Côte d'Ivoire. Proces d'Occidentalization*, Paris, 1981.
41. P.B. Clarke, Field Notes, Senegal, Casamance Region, April 1981.
42. R. Horton, *Africa 1971*, op. cit., and *Africa*, Vol.45, No 3, 1975, Vol. 45, No 4, 1975.
43. Ibid. 1971, p. 101.
44. Ibid., pp. 102-104.
45. Ibid., p. 102.
46. Ibid., pp. 104-105.
47. Ibid., p. 105.
48. S. Lukes, *Emile Durkheim*, London, 1973, pp. 483 ff.
49. Ibid.
50. H.J. Fisher, "Conversion Reconsidered: Some Historical Aspects of Religious Conversion in Black Africa", *Africa*, Vol. 43, No 1, January 1973, pp. 27-42.
51. M. Klein, *Islam and Imperialism in Senegal*, Edinburgh, 1968, chap. 11.
52. M. Echeruo, *Victorian Lagos*, London, 1977, pp. 80 ff.
53. M. Kingsley, *West African Studies* (3rd edition), introduction by J. Flint, London, 1964, p. 108.
54. I.R. Vanden Dreisen, "Some Observations on the Family Unit, Religion and the Practice of Polygyny in Ife Division of Western Nigeria", *Africa*, Vol 42, No 1, 1972.

Concluding Summary: Religion, Development and Identity.

Terence Ranger

Somebody said to me just before this talk, "Now we are going to discover what has *really* been happening during these four days!" But of course that is not what you are going to discover. What I shall say now will reveal rather what has been happening in my mind during the conference, and just as Africans listening to missionaries brought with them everything that had happened in their minds and imaginations before, so too the ideas I already possessed before the conference have no doubt determined what I have filtered out and what I have put in to this report. This will be very much an individual impression.

Certainly these four days have made me think much harder about certain questions than I have done before and have forced me to carry the approach which I had already developed a few steps further. I want to begin with the third word in the conference title - "Identity". This I found before the conference the most problematical, the most residual and the most easily dismissable of the title's three words. "Identity" seemed to have been put in just as a sop to vague ideas of African "personality" or "authenticity". After these four days I still find the word problematical, perhaps even more so than before, but it can obviously not be dismissed. It may even be true to say that as the conference has developed we have come to talk very much more about identity than we have about development; or perhaps it is more correct to say that we have come to define development in terms of identity, or of realisation of identity. So clearly at the end of the conference we need to think much more about the idea of identity. I must say that I am still inclined to express my scepticism about a good deal of what has been said during the conference about "identity", but I wish to do this in a reasonably systematic way. I did at one point in the proceedings think that perhaps I might escape from summing up at all by merely saying to you: "What I have learnt from this conference is that we ought not to impose linear classifi-cations upon the rich immediacies of African experience, and instead of making or listening to a report we should all rush out into the sun and continue to experience each other", but I'm afraid that linear classification has me in its grip.

It seems to me that from many of the things that have been said at the conference one can construct a straw-man, a set of propositions, which one could then proceed to demolish. I think in this case that the straw-man I am going to construct is not so unreal or unfair after all, and that you will recognise a set of propositions which really have emerged during our discussions. The following, then, are the propositions which I want to examine.

The first relates to Africa before colonialism. We have been told often during these four days that traditional African societies were communal, integrated and with no effective distinction between religion and society. So, for example, in Dr Moyo's paper he told us that "in traditional societies religion was not an affair of the individual, but was viewed as a matter for the entire community. Every member of the community was obliged to participate in the faith of the community. Religion permeated all aspects of African life, there was no separation between the sacred and the profane or between church and state". You will remember that he went on from that passage to suggest that the contemporary movement in Zimbabwe towards the one-party state, a one-credal nation, was a modern realisation of those traditional realities. Opposed to all this, we have been told, is the very different impact of the West. The impact of Western colonialism, of which Christianity can be seen as a major value-bearer, had, so it is argued, a disorienting effect on African societies, producing an increasingly intensified identity crisis in the towns, in the schools, in the churches, between men and women. In Europe and America themselves many people have be-moaned the effects of Western linearity, rationality and individualism; the separation of the public and private spheres; the separation of religion from the social/material sphere; the rise of technology and bureaucracy and the consequent stress, psychic problems, alienation, loneliness, dissolution of norms - in short, a great crisis of identity. In Africa, it has been argued, this crisis of identity was even more intense.

In Africa the very concept of time and sequence has been transformed; norms are disintegrating; the world is often felt to be chaotic. People have spoken of a crisis of split personalities. Such a polarised view of traditional communalism and integration on the one side and of modern disintegration on the other is expressed in much black theology. Black theology speaks of corporate personality in traditional Africa and of the heresy of individualistic capitalism in the twentieth century, eroding and breaking down traditional communalism, dominating, oppressing and creating profound human and societal sickness. The most striking expression, perhaps, of the profound sickness at the core of African society came from Professor Swantz when she said that the crisis of identity has affected those most basic of human relations, relations within the family, gender relations. Men are now, in her terms, "pseudo-guardians" of women and suffer from a consciousness of false identity which is extremely dangerous because such a consciousness generates loss of self-respect. Even more strikingly she asserted that "it is the false identity of African men on which Africa is now building its society".

Now I am not concerned to criticise Professor Swantz's propositions. She is clearly identifying a real crisis which occurs when groups or classes or genders justify their self-interested actions by reference to "tradition", but at the same time give in effect a totally different meaning to "traditional" relationships. But I *am* concerned to argue against the over-generalised statement of a modern African identity crisis. (After all, in Professor Swantz's case, the trouble is caused at least as much by a false estimation of so-called "tradition" as it is by the contemporary realities of social relationships). But before I deploy my counter-arguments it is necessary to go on to show the asserted connections which have been postulated at this conference, and elsewhere, between colonial capitalist change and religion.

It is asserted that *good* religion, healthy religion, founds identity in community. African "traditional" religion or the Coptic church in Ethiopia did this, we are told, by being co-existent with and inseparable from society. *Destructive* religion - mission Christianity, bearing Western values; mission Christianity as a dimension of what we are told on the first day of the conference was a cultural change on a hitherto unknown scale - threatens identities. Such religion breaks down the ideological solidarity of African societies. Moreover, as Peter Berger would argue[1], Western Christianity has itself been, ironically, the major secularising influence in twentieth century Africa.

There has been a further proposition argued at this conference which makes another sort of connection between the modern African identity crisis and religion. It was most clearly stated, I think, by Peter Clarke in the debate about Islamicisation, where he emphasised that identity crises are favourable to or precipitate religious change. You will remember that Dr Clarke disclaimed as a historian any possibility of focussing on the individual or the individual's crisis of spirituality. Nevertheless, the historian could explain religious change in terms of group or collective identity crisis. Situations of profound dislocation, circumstances that are perceived to be irredeemably evil, explain rapid movements of conversion. If you have lost confidence you look for something new.

All this seems to be a very radical attack on colonial capitalism and its ideologies. All this seems to offer a way of constructing theology which can take Africa back to organic solidarities and securities. And yet, and yet, I wonder. I think that we need to realise that so far from being new, re-volutionary propositions which undermine colonial understanding of Africa, the ideas of African traditional communalism versus Western individualism, the idea of the trauma of urbanisation, and so on were the very stereotypes of colonial social science. They are *not* intrinsically radical propositions. Such ideas underlay, for example, the whole colonial sociology of so called "urbanisation". The idea was that Africans coming to town from small-scale rural societies suffered a devastating identity crisis which meant that they could not really become true townsmen; which meant that they needed points of reference to construct some sort of feeling of identity, such as the de-liberate construction of "urban ethnicity", or membership in an African church. Moreover, colonial social science also extensively deployed the idea that religious change arouse out of identity crisis; that new religious move-ments were a compensation for deprivation.

There was certainly a time when I took these ideas very seriously myself. At various points in my Africanist career there has been one particular book that I wanted to press upon my protesting non-Africanist relatives so as to show them the *real* truth about Africa. Looking back I regard the sequence of such books as a map of what excited me at those moments - and of what I have come to think of now as essentially misleading. One such book was J.V. Taylor's *The Primal Vision*.[2] In that book there is a marvellous scene which for him represented the difference between collective African ex-perience and individual European experience; I think it was a scene of fisher-men on the shore of a lake, all pulling in their nets like parts of one great organism, all feeling exactly the same thing, with the missionary fisher of men out in the cold, merely watching and feeling individual. I did not at that time object to the word "primal" which somehow seemed to be not a bit like "primitive". So I made my relatives read *The Primal Vision* and I have not yet caught up with all those to whom I gave it to purify their understandings with my later illuminations!

The next such book that excited me was Colin Turnbull's *The Lonely African*.[3] Nowadays, and after his book on the Ik, we all know that we should not be excited by Turnbull - he has become the anthropological equivalent of a substance dangerous to the health. But I did not realise that in those days. I *was* excited by *The Lonely African* and for a long time I used to give it to friends. It is a marvellous work of art, like most of Turnbull's books, and I have come to believe that like most of them it is really about the lonely anthropologist. It presents a series of life histories, beautifully voiced by Zairean Africans, either traditionalists who no longer understand a world in which they are given no respect by the young, or by urban migrants who have no sense of identity. It is a profoundly melancholy book. I gave it to my relatives to make them properly melancholy; to make them understand what their civilisation had done to Africans.

Now colonialism certainly did very many brutal and shameful things. But I began to be very suspicious of the book. It has no apparatus; Turnbull does not tell us whether the life histories are transcribed from interviews; and in the end I concluded that they are works of art, fictions. No other African testimony I have ever come across has this dignified, keening, mourning note that characterises these statements. Africans in Zaire had plenty to lament but *these* are Turnbull's lamentations. Real Zairean testimonies, such as those being collected by John Higginson of the University of Illinois, are much more turbulent and assertive. I became suspicious of *The Primal Vision* too, and that book as well came to seem representative more of the sensibility and aspirations of the author than of the realities of African religious consciousness.

Since I first read these books I have come to look more closely at pre-colonial Africa and pre-colonial religion - and all those traditional Africans who ought to be living in single-minded religious collectivity don't in fact look like that at all. There seems instead to have been a great pluralism and openness and heterodoxy. And I have come to look more closely at colonial social history where all those Africans who ought to be terribly atomised and lonely certainly don't seem that way. When one sees African migrants in the colonial towns, where they were certainly oppressed and pushed around, they nevertheless seem resilient and gregarious and adaptable. I approve of the shift in African urban social history from the old studies of anomie and trauma to the new emphasis on African participation in a struggle for the city.[4] Indeed, I have myself written a paper, with one of my favourite alliterative titles - it is called "Pugilism and Pathology" - which is about African boxing and colonial sociology in Salisbury, Southern Rhodesia, in the late 1930s. The Chief Native Commissioner was terribly worried about African boxing. In fact he was terribly worried about African urbanisation altogether. He feared that the closed corporate communities of the rural areas were breaking down and that coming to town was a shattering experience for Africans, reducing them to a clinically pathological state. African boxing matches seemed to him to symbolise all this. It was not an *African* sport, but a proletarian one. Yet neither was it conducted in a European way. Nobody ever knocked anyone else out, for example, and there were no timed rounds and no points and nobody ever won. African boxers came into the ring, and danced about, and showed off to the crowd, and there was a flurry of blows, and then one of the boxers, feeling tired, would lean against the ropes while his opponent danced some more. I was fascinated to see that the Chief Native Commissioner was at least as worried by this lack of purposeful violence in the ring as he was by the potential for fighting between supporters of the boxers outside it. The sociologist appointed to investigate this worrying boxing concluded that it was indeed typical of what happened when Africans came to town - they lost their own sports and merely mimicked European ones. They ape the gestures of boxing, he said, but they lack its sociology! So there was a great debate on what to do about it. The Chief Native Commissioner wanted to ban boxing altogether and maybe to encourage tribal dancing. But he was persuaded by the Social Welfare officers that instead an attempt should be made to introduce Africans to the "sociology of boxing", and there followed hilarious scenes where white administrators literally dangled boxing gloves over the heads of urban Africans as instruments of social control. African boxers were given proper gloves if they fought in a system of rounds and points - but this caused more riots because the spectators thought it so unfair that a man could be hit while resting upon the ropes! All this solemn absurdity arose from the idea that coming to town blew an African's mind, literally, and that lonely Africans flocked to meaningless recreations. Meanwhile there positively springs out of the data the marvellous, cheerful adaptations to urban life, the innovation of new structures of fraternity and association, the evolution of an urban popular culture.[5]

This story of colonial Salisbury even while illustrating my point has drawn me away from the main thrust of my argument which is that the propositions about identity crisis made at this conference can and have to be challenged. Take the proposition about pre-colonial, small-scale, integrated unities of religion and politics. I just do not believe that this was generally true. African religion was not in this sense unitary, but plural, multi-layered and often in structural opposition to political authority. I can draw here upon one of the comments of Bishop Patrick Kalilombe in his discussion of Dr Moyo's paper. Kalilombe made a very important distinction between village level religion and the level of the wider, regional territorial shrines which seek to manage land and ecology. Much of what he said showed these territorial shrines in conflict with the state, and here he was not talking about the colonial state. He was talking about the religious and political history of pre-colonial Central Africa where successive states tried to control the various layers of religion. They could not really do that at the village level, but they could do it - or try to do it - at the level of the regional cult. I say "try to do it", because states did not always succeed. Thus the "High God cult" with which Dr Moyo began his paper - the Mwari or Mlimo cult - was never identical with any African state in its zone of influence, and never completely subordinated politically. Its zone of influence overlapped with several successive African states - with what we call the Torwa, the Rozwi and the Ndebele - just as it overlapped the colonial boundaries of Rhodesia, Bechuanaland and Mozambique. It had its own apparatus of tribute and its own internal politics. So the real history of the High God cult has lessons different from those asserted by Dr Moyo. I don't know whether this real history might lead us to argue for multi-party rather than one-party states, but it might at least lead us to favour a pluralism in which there are church networks as well as state networks.[6]

I can also draw upon the comments of Agnes Chepkwony in the discussion of Peter Clarke's paper. Clarke had given examples of change and discontinuity, of people rushing off and burning their idols. But Agnes objected that surely this did not mark a new era of divisiveness in contrast to past unities. Surely, she said, African religions themselves contained the possibilities of these sort of transformations. And indeed she was right. A great deal of historical research on African religion, especially in Central Africa, has revealed a recurrent sequence of movements of revitalisation and of challenge to the authority of established religion, something like subsequent movements of Christian Revival. These revitalisation movements involved great bonfires of charms and amulets - a repudiation of everything which up to that moment had been protective and revered.[7]

I am merely restating here points I have argued over the years - that African religions were complex, multi-layered, dynamic, with a history of contradiction, contestation, innovation. I would wish to replace the model of the total organic collectivity with something else - a model of creative and resilient pluralism; a model which helps to explain the remarkable adaptability of African societies and individuals during the changes of colonial capitalism. If we take, for example, a man living in the savannah belt of pre-colonial Africa. He did not have one single identity expressed by one single, shared religion. He had numerous different identities lived out in relationships with numerous different "persons" and expressed in different layers of religious belief and ritual. One male identity is that of son or husband or father expressed through and legitimated in the ancestral cult of the village or clan. Another male identity is that of the cultivator, or director of family agricultural production, and here the relationship expressed in religious observance is that with the land, as personified in the spirits of the regional territorial cult. As the man goes on pilgrimage to the cult centre so he becomes part of a different and wider community than that of the village, clan or chiefdom. Another identity of the same man is that of hunter or craftsman and here neither the ancestral nor the territorial cults dominate. As hunter the man may belong to distinct hunters' guilds or cults of the forest, where he is linked with non-kin in quite separate rites and practices. The same man might also go as porter or trader and travel far outside the boundaries even of the territorial cult, and need to express his relations with the alien peoples among whom he travelled. Then this same man, who belongs to an ancestral cult, and a territorial cult and a hunters' guild, can also become a member of a cult of spirit possession by extra-social, non-kin, amoral spirits of affliction. There is a marvellous book by John Janzen about the development of a "drum of affliction" north of the river Zaire. The cult is called Lemba and Janzen shows that there was a transition in Loango from a period in which the king was able to control trade and production and where ancestral and earth cults were crucial, to a period where royal authority broke down and there arose a much wider trading system of diffused exchange. What then happened was the growth of the Lemba cult of affliction, a marvellously African concept. Its members were brought together by consciousness of shared affliction; they were thought to suffer the same disease, caused by the same spirit; they were initiated into Lemba by recognising that spirit. Across a very large zone Lemba knitted together the traders and caravan leaders and producers in a new religious expression of identity, bringing them together in the idiom of the shared affliction of being prosperous and thus attracting the malevolence of the needy.[8]

The various cultic layers to which my hypothetical man belonged did not fit neatly together to form one single collective religion co-existent with one policy or society. Moreover, even when my man - or a hypothetical woman for that matter - remained in the local community and was not away as pilgrim, hunter or trader, stranger diviners and prophets and witchcraft eradicators regularly passed through, offering new religious ideas and solutions, to which my man responded with all the curiosity and enthusiasm of someone for whom the exotic carries a particular religious authority. How different all this is from the organic model of the identity of society, state, collectivity, religion. And yet I am sure it is more accurate. The local community was of course tremendously important, but it was situated in these various networks of symbolic and practical recourse.

Now, if this *is* a more accurate picture of pre-colonial Central Africa, or East Africa, then the impact of Christianity and colonialism is likely to have been rather different from the notion of a fatal smashing of secure corporate identity. If I am right, then African religions were already adept at reflecting and expressing multiple identities and African "believers" were already experienced in responding to new religious ideas. If I am right people were familiar with the balance of tensions *within* African religions and between them and the state. If I am right people were already familiar with sweeping economic, political *and* religious change. Hence they were not nearly so defenceless against the impact of colonial capitalism and "individualistic" Christianity as we often imagine. I am encouraged in these prejudices by Doctor Farias' presentation here on West African Islam. As I understood him he was arguing that many West African societies were constituted by a functioning balance of opposites, "traditional" religion and Islam. But he also suggested that such a balance of opposites had not been brought into being by the arrival of Islam. Rather the tension between distinct religious principles had existed within "traditional" religion before the arrival of Islam, and its existence gave Islam an opportunity to enter. Professor Rubenson asserted in conference discussion that in Ethiopia, too, there had been a fundamental tension between the constituent parts of Coptic Christianity, and he added that "there is something in the African soil which engenders pluralism". I also think that the African soil nurtured flexibility of identity and of its religious expression. Tribal or ethnic identity, for instance, was greatly more flexible, less defined, than it has become in twentieth century Africa.

Hence I think that mission Christianity too could enter African societies, like Farias' West African Islam, as a part of a system of balanced opposites; that Christian expressions of identity could be drawn upon to express new and additional layers of experience and self-definition such as becoming a peasant or becoming a worker. Things didn't just "fall apart" with the coming of colonialism. *Of course*, colonialism has been brutally alienating; in the most literal sense people have been expropriated, their land has been taken, their identities have been manipulated. But Africans have been much less bewildered than we often imagine, much better able to negotiate new identities and to express them in religious terms.

So far as African peasantries are concerned this was the whole point of my own paper to this conference. But Africans can turn themselves into town workers as well as into peasants. Bengt Sundkler in his presentation to this conference emphasised the religious vitality of the towns and I am sure that he will show in his forthcoming book the creative use of religion to establish urban African identities.

So the African identity crisis has not been so general or so profound as is often asserted. If we are going to employ in any useful way the concept of identity crisis we have to be much more particular. It is not much use talking about such a crisis affecting all Africans over a hundred years. We have to ask ourselves under what circumstances is there really trauma, power-lessness, a collapse of all values?

One such extreme circumstance was discussed a good deal at the conference - the plight of the refugee. Professor Sundkler emphasised the refugee as one of the major figures of his book on the Christian Movement in Africa; Patrick Kalilombe told us that Archbishop Milingo, uprooted from his healing mission in Zambia, has now been made responsible not only for tourists but for refugees. Professor Rubenson very movingly described the Coptic missionary in Ethiopia as a wandering refugee, never staying long in one place. All these references pointed towards the theological significance of the refugee - the poorest of the poor, the incarnation of Christ, yet also free and open to inspiration, not only a standing reproach to a fat-cat church but also a promise of painful rebirth.

Let me turn back for a moment to Zimbabwe. My own paper was about peasants who stayed on the land where they were and because of all the local spiritual resources and their capacity to draw on religious pluralism managed to survive a terrible war. But what happened to those who did not stay where they were but fled to the towns or to Mozambique? Bengt Sundkler has drawn my attention to a crisis of identity among refugee women in the towns by lending to me the *Jesuit Yearbook* for 1984. This contains an account of work done in 1979, in the last year of the war in Zimbabwe, in a township called Chitungwiza, near Harare, which was crammed with refugees from the countryside. The author of the account is Brother Chishiri, a black Jesuit, who was assigned by the black Catholic Archbishop to work with these refugees. I was enormously struck when reading his account of how he healed the traumas of refugee women by its similarities with the healing sessions of Archbishop Milingo as these were described to us by Patrick Kalilombe. Milingo liberates people from the identity confusion caused by spirit possession. Chishiri liberated refugee women from their own identity confusion caused by what had happened on the death of their husbands. The husbands had been executed by guerillas during the war; their bodies had been left unburied; neither the wives nor any other villagers had been allowed to mourn them. These women had been unable to release their grief; they felt separated from society and culture through their failure to give their husbands a proper burial. Chishiri and his eight dedicated Catholic mothers moved into the refugee camps to find people who "were lonely indeed" - and not with the stagy loneliness of Colin Turnbull's Africans. The refugees were "people who had lost hope, for whom life had become meaningless, people with big wounds that none could heal, but only God himself". Chishiri began to try to work among these people, but it became intolerable to him, just as it became intolerable to Archbishop Milingo, to see the suffering of the afflicted. "Every evening when I got back to my little camping room and tried to look back on the day or tried to say the Divine Office, which I love, I could only see the faces of mothers with tears in their eyes for whom I had not the time to say a word of consolation. Trying to think was a nightmare."

By this time Chishiri himself was in a crisis of identity and it is fascinating to see how he dealt with it. He developed a Retreat in three stages - lamentation, sharing, forgiveness. He brought together the war widows and Catholics from Harare and he began the release of tension. "This part", he warns us, "is very emotional". A moment of silence, followed by floods of tears, shouting, getting the stored-up anger out - very much like the first stages of a Milingo exorcism. "It is time to be ourselves, time to sing, time to cry". Then he says that if these women had lost their husbands in traditional society everyone in the community would have come round and shared in their lamentations and cried with them, and they would have been able to talk about their grief, there would have been a thunder of noise. So in the next stage he and the Harare women reconstructed community mourning for the widows, sitting down with them, crying and shouting and howling, and after that talking with them about their husbands. Then came the third stage, that of integration. Guilt, anger, sadness had been poured out; the women were then asked to forgive themselves for their thoughts of despair and of suicide. Finally everyone helped them formulate plans for the future.

I found all this enormously impressive - and how fascinating it would be if Archbishop Milingo in his mission to refugees were to meet Brother Chishiri in a refugee camp and they could compare their varying ways of dealing with extreme crises of identity. I have shared this with you because here we clearly do have a case of identity crisis and we also have a striking example of the part religion can play in resolving it. But even at this level, the level of the displaced refugee, this is not the only point to make. The helplessness of such people, their inability to relieve their own suffering, these are not the only things to note. Nor are they the only things that Jesuits have noted about refugees. While Brother Chishiri was working with these

people in Salisbury, young white Jesuits were simultaneously living in refugee camps in Zambia and Mozambique, and they were neither healing nor
counselling nor serving mass. They were just there, sharing the experience
of those refugees. The then Jesuit General, Father Arrupe, has presented an
important document on the theological implication of these refugees. And he
writes that "these people became for us a symbol of hope". In those camps
in Zambia and in Mozambique the refugees formed new communities, and
especially new communities of hope. They were so much more hopeful than
the Jesuits who were living among them.

So even in this most extreme of cases, we would go sadly astray if we
thought of these Africans solely as victims. And I think that this example
helps us to be more exact than we have been in determining where the really
crucial, criminal deprivations of identity have taken place. For these
Zimbabwean refugees there was a recourse. The ones in the towns could be
reintegrated, healed by the reenactment of their rural culture. The ones in the
camp could be healed by history-based reflection on their future. But what
about people who do not have such recourse, whose only available culture
has lost a healing capacity, for whom history is a trap?

Per Frostin drew our attention particularly to South Africa and if we look
at South Africa then we begin to understand how acute an identity crisis can
be. It is significant that of all the regimes in the world South Africa is the
one most concerned with identity. The whole apartheid policy is concerned
with allocation of identity - who is white, who is black, who is Zulu, who is
Pondo. It is an identity obsessed regime. So we can hardly accuse it of
destroying identities. But what we *can* accuse it of is having frozen identities. The real identity crisis in Africa is *not* found in changes from a single
traditional "frozen" identity to a bewildering pluralism. The real identity
crisis is exactly the other way round. It is produced by the change from a
creative pluralism to single frozen identities. These are people who have
been allotted a single identity - no matter what they do or where they go they
are Zulu, or a Pondo.

What the South African government has done is a great crime. It has
poisoned the past. There are hardly any black South African historians
because black South Africans cannot bear to look at history. These people
cannot use their past because it has been frozen into a cluster of single
identities, of closed communities. Because of the official folk ethnography
that has flourished in South Africa, with its emphasis on "tribal" solidarity,
what has happened has been the denial of possibility, the denial of
pluralism, the denial of flexibility. I think that although one can see this most
clearly in South Africa one can see it happening also in other places. You

will recall that after Dr Farias' paper on West African Islam the chair-person remarked that while he was talking about a tolerant, open Islam, elsewhere, and even within Nigeria itself, we were witnessing the rise of an exclusively defined Islam with a narrow fanaticism. And Professor Rubenson told us that it would be impossible now in Ethiopia to have the old interactions and intermarriages between Christians and Moslems. Or consider the emergence of "tribe" as a dominant identifying factor, not only in South Africa but in many other places too. Hence one of the greatest problems of identity is that in too many parts of Africa it is being so narrowly defined that the flexibility of identity that existed in the past has been circumscribed.

Let me turn quickly to development. Here at least there has been little disagreement between us. By development we all seem to mean the same thing - self-development by the poor, from out of their communities - so we have talked about basic needs, basic communities, taking the side of the poor, the village church, and so on. All of us, development advisers, historians, liberation theologians, guerrillas, the representatives of the Ujamaa state are going out to and working with rural and urban communities. So far so good. If there has been among us an advocate of the necessity for ruthless and sweeping macro-economic change that advocate has remained very silent. So we have all agreed, but there still remains an instrumental question: "How much of what we agree on is going to do the poor any good?" I cannot help feeling that there are really disturbing problems in this. Professor Swantz dramatised in her talk the extent to which development schemes almost invariably over-ride local perceptions, no matter what detailed research has been done, no matter how often developers are told about the necessity of taking into account the perceptions and needs of women. In such a situation our own research and our own activity sometimes seems merely to have lent a spurious ideological legitimacy to the action of the state. As Professor Swantz said, there is a great temptation to think that people would be better off left alone. Bishop Kalilombe hinted that states, whether capitalist or socialist, make much the same demands, and in particular that, however much they may call for lively local communities or basic communities of radical theology, they do not much like them when they appear. It will be a real test to see how President Banana and the Zimbabwean state will react to the local "communities of promise" which his theology calls for. In most places governments and ruling parties do not like autonomous communities of promise.

So one is really tempted to think that local communities are best left alone not only by developers but also by the state. I have even had the heretical thought this week that they might be best left alone by theologians as well. I have often said, and I still believe, that much of so-called "African theology", particularly "authenticity theology", is extremely authoritarian in its implications, a deliberate narrowing of identity and closing of plural and lively options. Look at the fruits of authenticity in Zaire. In the name of authenticity only the great big bureaucratic churches are allowed to operate. In the name of authenticity the Kimbanguists have hidden the Holy Spirit and got a constitution and operate like a bureaucracy, whereas all the real "authentic" religious movements, in all their rich variety and chaos, are frowned on and sometimes persecuted. As for Black Theology even in its most attractive form - and Bishop Kalilombe's presentation last night was certainly its most attractive form - one cannot help asking, what then follows when we have listened to the cry of the slave, of the oppressed? The articulation of this cry constitutes only the first stage of the sort of therapy that Archbishop Milingo or Brother Chishiri practice. When the agony has been heard what can be done about it? How can you show the people that theology is any use to them to go beyond expressing that cry and into the stages of reconciliation and reintegration? Sometimes I wonder whether there is not a sort of very basic liberation prayer going up from the villages of Africa - "From developers, government agents, churchmen and theologians, Good Lord deliver us".

Yet of course one cannot give way to this romantic choice of the locals against the outsiders. As Professor Swantz has said, no matter how "uncaptured" the peasantry are, they *are* encapsulated and their choices can only be made within the context of the forces that affect them. In my own paper I quoted an early colonial American missionary, in all his complacency, saying that "the great problem is the problem of poverty, poverty of material comfort, poverty of social ideals, poverty of religious conceptions. Richness must be poured into their lives". Give and take the language, that is what Banana is saying too. Despite everything that I argue in my paper - don't be so patronising; these people have done very well for themselves - of course this poverty remains a fundamental truth. Turning oneself into a peasant, even if this is a heroic and necessary thing to do, nevertheless produces introverted lives. Just look at Scandinavia. Everywhere I have been I have seen museums of peasant life and art; peasant culture is a great comfort to you now that you do not have to be peasants, but these museums body forth very narrow lives. My peasants in Makoni, who were a great source of inspiration and comfort to me, when I only had to visit them every so often, lead in most cases very constricted lives. Plainly they should be given richness. But the question, of course, is how you do it. You clearly cannot give them richness by just assuming that they would be richer if they thought like you do. One cannot impose richness on people. What you have to do is to create facilities - ideological and practical - which they can use to expand.

Moreover it is true that in local communities of hope, which Zimbabwe still has in abundance, peasants do not actually want to be left alone. Researchers who have been talking to Zimbabwean peasants have been struck by their naivety. The peasants are saying "We want government assistance, we want help to grow our crops and to market them". "How naive", says the researcher, "these peasants do not realise that you cannot get government assistance without government interference". Well, if the peasants in Zimbabwe do not know that they must be really naive because they have experienced so many decades of colonial government interference. Today they have the hope that "the theology of promise" means that the government will assist them but not coerce them. They want assistance and what one sees is that the choice is not between community and bureaucracy but between fruitful rather than destructive relationships of community and outsiders. One has got to try to find structures and ideas which will enable the pouring of richness into local communities, and I know that this is what the best liberation theology is about.

I found the panel on independent churches yesterday enormously enlightening so far as this question is concerned. We began with the usual contrast - the small-scale independent church, congregations of no more than two hundred, as contrasted to the historic mission churches with their great international bureaucratic apparatus, their resources but also their bureaucratic sterility. The independent churches seem to have advantages of organic life but disadvantages of impoverished resources. But I do not think that this contrast is where we ended.

We began to talk about Bengt Sundkler's word "structures". He said, "Oh, how I love that word; but don't ask an old man to define what it means". Well, we were too kind. Not only did we not ask him but we did not really ever ask ourselves either, and it seems to me that we now need to do so. When Professor Hallencreutz said that there are some structures which are useful and life-giving as well as some that are stiflingly bureaucratic, one might have suspected that this was merely the Uppsala tradition speaking again. But in fact it seems to me to be true. We began to discuss in that panel why it was that some remarkable black clergymen remained in the mainline churches despite all the humiliations. Was it because they wanted the great tradition? Yes, but also because most churches possessed structures that despite everything could be used to help people.

When I was researching myself into the churches during the Zimbabwean guerrilla war I was drawn to conclude that the contrast was not really between the local community and the distant structures of the hierarchy. Many people have concluded that the war showed that autonomous local communities can act much more creatively than hierarchies and structures. Yet the "holy men" I wrote about[9] - the Irish Carmelite priests and the black Anglican ones - were able to be wonder-working holy men for their communities not only because they possessed local legitimacy but also because they could pick up the phone and speak to the Bishop's secretary in Harare and make sure that people arrested one day had a lawyer the next. They could serve their communities because they could draw on the structures.

So the contrast is not between communal vitality and structural rigidity. What we have to do is ask more insistently what kind of structures can themselves be vital, and what sort of relations should exist between them and local communities. After all, when we were looking at the independent churches we came to realise that they too are not content with organic small-ness of scale. I spoke then about the *Vapostori* (Apostolic) churches. Though these originated in eastern Zimbabwe in rural areas, both the Masowe and the Maranke *Vapostori* are now international churches. They have spread throughout Central Africa and they have become rather like traditional religion, at once the focus of local community and a network along which people can travel. A rooted belonging, but also this astonishing network. Professor Rubenson argued that the same had been true for Ethiopian Orthodoxy - astonishing pluralism, vitality, localism, but all comprehended within a loose network of identity and resource. One emerged from the seminar on independent churches with a vision, at least as utopian no doubt as those I have been criticising. We noticed some con-tinuities between pre-colonial and colonial structures, continuities precisely in terms of flexibility and pluralism. A balance between the local and the network structures of religion, enriching resources available to people, cutting across limiting identities - a utopian vision, indeed.

Finally, I want to say a few words about something we have not actually discussed at all. What are the implications of all this for what the churches actually do? By this I mean "what can the sending churches actually do?" This, after all, is the question most relevant to most people here. However much we agree that local, grassroots initiatives in Africa are the key, *we* cannot bring those about. Now, I have come to think that if there is - and we have seen that there is - a specifically religious contribution to resolving problems of identity and development, then perhaps we should review the policies of the sending churches. They have committed themselves so far to projects of material development and very properly withdrawn from a merely pious evangelism. And of course I understand why. Bishop Kalilombe yesterday told us that people's identity is a matter for themselves and that they now say to the churches that no scheme from above, no matter how subtle its adaptation theology, can do it for them. People begin to say, no, no, this is not it. Now we must really be ourselves. And he talked about the cost of this, of becoming essentially an independent church without calling on the resources of those who have been your partners or masters in the past. I accept this entirely and I accept equally the need for the men of the Church to be with the poor and not to live at a higher standard of living. And yet is it essential for so many of the churches in Africa to be so poor?

Take one example with which I am slightly familiar - the Anglican church in southern Tanzania. It is desperately poor. It is in no state to pour richness into anyone's lives. The African priests in southern Tanzania get less than the basic minimum wage. Their congregations are so poor that they cannot support them, still less support the intellectual work of the church, its theological training. The African clergy have no space to develop a relevant theology of richness; they have no libraries except mouldering volumes of *Punch* inherited from their UMCA missionary predecessors. Can this be right? Can that church enrich the lives of its people? What does world Anglicanism think it is up to? Yes, of course you should put money into pumping water. But should you not also put money into libraries and theological schools? Not of course with the aim of making the Anglican church in southern Tanzania a Church Triumphant and not of course in the spirit of saying "My God, the Anglicans are losing out to Islam in the south, we had better get another canon down there". But in the spirit of everything I have been talking about, of pluralism of ideas, flexibility of identity, the possibility of becoming a resource for local enrichment. It seems to me that the sending churches have a responsibility for the African churches which have grown out of them and that this responsibility can surely be met without patronage.

Of course, it is right to abandon the idea that the mission of the church is a purely spiritual one, quite separate from economic and social and political change. But is it right to abandon the idea that the role of the church is to ensure that spiritual richness accompanies economic and social development? Is there not a specifically religious contribution to problems of identity and development? Should not those initiatives of the local churches which promise spiritual enrichment be supported? If we need networks of resource then the African churches have to be assisted in developing resources. You will realise that I am not talking about giving support, moral and financial, to attempts to create closed corporate Anglican - or any other - communities. Quite the contrary. I am talking about enabling alternative networks of identity and resource to thrive; of fostering creative pluralism. In so many African countries church networks are the only alternatives to the networks of party and state, and it is of crucial importance that they be there, not so they should oppose the state, but as alternative sources of identity. For without alternatives the realisation of identity can become crippling rather than liberating.

NOTES

1. Peter L. Berger, *The Social Reality of Religion* , Faber and Faber, London, 1969. For an application of this idea to Africa see Terence Ranger, 'Secularisation in Twentieth Century Africa', in "History and Humanism", *New Edinburgh Review*, 38/39, Summer-Autumn 1977.
2. John V. Taylor, *The Primal Vision. Christian Presence Amid African Religion* , SCM Press, London, 1963.
3. Colin M. Turnbull, *The Lonely African*, Simon and Schuster, New York, 1962.
4. Frederick Cooper, ed., *Struggle for the City*, Sage, London, 1983.
5. My paper is to appear in a collection *Sport in Africa*, edited by J.A. Mangan.
6. J.M. Schoffeleers ed., *Guardians of the Land*, Mambo Press, Gwelo, 1978.
7. John M. Janzen, "The Tradition of Renewal in Kongo Religion", in Neville S. Booth ed., *African Religions*, Nok, London, 1977.
8. John M. Janzen, *Lemba, 1650 - 1930: A Drum of Affliction in Africa and the New World*, Garland, New York, 1982.
9. Terence Ranger, "Holy Men and rural communities in Zimbabwe, 1970 to 1980", in W. Sheils, ed., *The Church and War*, Blackwells, Oxford, 1983.

NOTES ON CONTRIBUTORS

Peter B Clarke is a lecturer at King's College, University of London. His published work includes *West Africa and Islam*, Arnold, London, 1982 and *A History of Christianity in West Africa*, Arnold, London, 1984.

Carl Fredrik Hallencreutz is professor of missiology at the University of Uppsala. He is currently a visiting professor in the Department of Religious Studies and Philosophy at the University of Zimbabwe. His published works include *Nigerian Negotiations: A Study in the Search for Church Union in Nigeria*, Uppsala, 1967, and *Till Alla Folk*, Proprius, Stockholm, 1985.

Emefie Ikenga-Metuh is a lecturer in the Department of Religious Studies, University of Jos, Nigeria. He was a guest lecturer at the Faculty of Theology at the University of Uppsala during the spring term 1984.

Ambrose M Moyo is a lecturer at the Department of Religious Studies and Philosophy at the University of Zimbabwe.

Ludvig Munthe is professor of Missiology and History of Religions at the Free Faculty of Theology (Church of Norway), Oslo. His published work includes *Deux Manuscrits Arabico-Malgache en Provenance de Londre*, Tananarive, 1975, and *La Tradition Arabico-Malgache vue à travers le Manuscrit A6 d'Oslo et d'autres Manuscrits disponibles*, Oslo, 1982.

Terence Ranger is professor of modern history at the Victoria University of Manchester. His publications include *Revolt in Southern Rhodesia, 1896-97*, Heinemann, London, 1979, and *Peasant Consciousness and Guerilla War in Zimbabwe*, Heinemann, London, 1984.

Jarle Simensen is professor of history at the University of Trondheim. His publications include *Studieplan om Afrika*, Den Norske Nationalkommisjon for Unesco, Oslo, 1966.

Bengt Sundkler is professor emeritus at the Faculty of Theology, University of Uppsala and has served as a Bishop in the Bukoba diocese of the Evangelical Lutheran Church of Tanzania. His published work includes *Bantu Prophets in South Africa*, OUP, London, 1961 and *Zulu Zions and some Swazi Zionists*, Gleerups/OUP, Lund, 1976.

Marja-Liisa Swantz is director of the Institute of Development Studies at the University of Helsinki. Her publications include *Women in Development: A Creative Role Denied?* C Hurst and Company, London, 1985.